DEEP RIVER

DEEP RIVER

AND

THE
NEGRO SPIRITUAL
SPEAKS OF LIFE
AND DEATH

by
Howard Thurman

RICHMOND

INDIANA

Library of Congress Number 75-27041
ISBN 0-913408-20-4

Copyright 1975 by Howard Thurman
Published 1975 by Friends United Press
Reprint 1990

General Introduction

The reprinting of *Deep River* and *The Negro Spiritual Speaks of Life and Death* in a single volume at this time may call for an explanation. All through the intervening years since the mid-forties when they first appeared, there has been an intermittent but consistent demand for them. This demand was greatly intensified during the period marked by a fresh sense of root or collective self-awareness brought into sharp focus by the tempests of the Civil Rights Movement. Despite the primary secular and political character of the movement it found sources of inspiration and courage in the spiritual insights that had provided a windbreak for our forefathers against the brutalities of slavery and the establishing of a ground of hope undimmed by the contradictions which held them in tight embrace. Often those who were most involved in the throes of the struggle were not aware of the dimension of this flow of courage from the past; nevertheless, it was a brooding presence in myriad rallies in a thousand churches which gave refuge and support to young and old in the heights and depths of the agonies of the '60s.

Many of my young friends have queried me at one critical point. Why is there so little attention given to the part that protest and resistance played in the life of our forefathers as expressed in the Spirituals? It is in order to state quite frankly, that initially these essays were addressed to a generation which tended to be ashamed of the Spirituals or who joined in the degrading and prostituting of the songs as a part of conventional minstrelsy or naive amusement exploited and capitalized by white entertainers. The aim was to denigrate and casually to humiliate. It seemed urgent to me to explore the ground of hope and self-respect in the idiom of the Spirituals. The element of protest was recognized in my exploration but was not emphasized. This seemed to me to make their timelessness more readily available to meet the new urgencies of that generation and, in my judgment, of subsequent generations.

My first formal statement of the religious significance of these songs was a series of chapel addresses to the students at Morehouse and Spelman Colleges in the academic year 1929-30. Six years earlier, during my senior year in college, there was an incident that precipitated my reflection upon the *meaning* of the Spirituals. A small party of visitors from the General Education Board was presented in chapel. After their minor greetings to us, on cue, the director of Music walked to the front and gave the key for the student who led the Spirituals. The student sang the first line and normally, the whole student body would come in with the body of the text as the swell of a great organ. But we did not respond. This was repeated — no response. The President of the college was embarrassed profoundly. In the evening, a special assembly was called and the entire student body was soundly reprimanded. The response to him was very simple. "We refuse to sing our songs to delight and amuse white people. The songs are ours and a part of the source of our own inspiration transmitted to us by our forefathers."

Finally, these essays are intimate and personal. They lay bare in my hand the gift which these songs, centuries old, are to my own spirit. For me, they are watering places for my own spirit and have enabled me to affirm life when its denial would be more ego satisfying, to honor my own heritage and rejoice in it.

> "To stay in the field
> To stay in the field
> Until the war is ended."

To My Sister Madeline

PROLOGUE

In 1945 I published privately a little volume of reflections on the religious insights of certain of the Negro spirituals. These reflections were first given as addresses before various groups. This early volume has long since been out of print, and as a result of many requests the manuscript has been revised and enlarged, and is now being re-issued under the same title.

My own life has been so deeply influenced by the genius of the spirituals that the meaning as distilled into my experience in my early years spills over in much that I have come to think in my maturity. The reader who is acquainted with *Jesus and the Disinherited* or with the Ingersoll lecture on "The Immortality of Man" under the title *The Negro Spiritual Speaks of Life and Death* will recognize at once some of the basic ideas expressed in this volume. For this I make no apology. In what is written here there is at work the movement of the creative spirit of God as it has sought under great odds to tutor my rebellious spirit in conflict with some of the tragedies of my social experience. I believe, with my forefathers, that this is God's world. This faith has had to fight against disillusionment, despair, and the vicissitudes of American history.

If some light may be thrown on the reader's struggle for courage, self-respect, and emotional security, no greater justification for publishing these reflections may be found. It is in this hope and with this spirit that they are sent on their way.

H. T.

I
CONCERNING
BACKGROUNDS

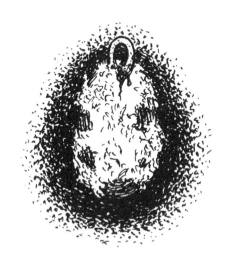

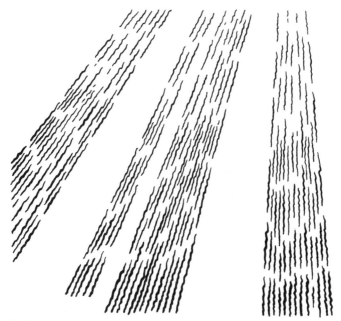

THE ante-bellum Negro preacher was the greatest single factor in determining the spiritual destiny of the slave community. He it was who gave to the masses of his fellows a point of view that became for them a veritable Door of Hope. His ministry was greatly restricted as to movement, function, and opportunities of leadership, but he himself was blessed with one important insight: he was convinced that every human being was a child of God. This belief included the slave as well as the master. When he spoke to his group on an occasional Sabbath day, he knew what they had lived through during the weeks; how their total environment had conspired to din into their minds and spirits the corroding notion that as human beings they were of no significance. Thus his one message springing full grown from the mind of God repeated in many ways a wide range of variations: "You are created in God's image. You are not slaves, you are not 'niggers'; you are God's children." Many weary, spiritually and physically exhausted slaves found new strength and power gushing up into all the reaches of their personalities, inspired by the words that fell from this man's lips. He had discovered that which religion insists is the ultimate truth about human life and destiny. It is the supreme validation of the human spirit. He who knows this is able to transcend the vicissitudes of life, however terrifying, and look out on the world with quiet eyes.

It is out of this sense of being a child of God that the genius of the religious folk songs is born. There were three major sources from which the raw materials of Negro spirituals were derived: the Old and New Testaments, the world of nature, and the personal experiences of religion that were the common lot of the people, emerging from their inner life. Echoes from each source are present in practically all the songs. We shall examine each of these somewhat in detail, with reference to the use to which they were put and the end result.

The Bible—Old Testament. The Christian Bible furnished much of the imagery and ideas with which the slave singers fashioned their melodies. There is great strength in the assurance that may come to a people that they are children of destiny. The Jewish concept of life as stated in their records made a profound impression on this group of people, who were themselves in bondage. God was at work in all history: He manifested himself in certain specific acts that seemed to be over and above the historic process itself.

The slave caught the significance of this truth at once. He sang:

> When Israel was in Egypt's land,
> Let my people go;
> Oppressed so hard they could not stand,
> Let my people go;

Refrain:

> Go down, Moses, 'way down in Egypt's land;
> Tell ole Pharaoh
> Let my people go.

> "Thus saith the Lord," bold Moses said,
> Let my people go;
> If not, I'll smite your first-born dead,
> Let my people go.

> No more shall they in bondage toil,
> Let my people go;
> Let them come out with Egypt's spoil,
> Let my people go.

The Lord told Moses what to do,
   Let my people go;
To lead the children of Israel thro'
   Let my people go.

When they had reached the other shore,
   Let my people go;
They sang a song of triumph o'er,
   Let my people go.

The experience of Daniel and his miraculous deliverance was also an ever-recurring theme:

My Lord delivered Daniel,
My Lord delivered Daniel,
My Lord delivered Daniel,
Why can't He deliver me?

The experiences of frustration and divine deliverance, as set forth in the stories of the Hebrews in bondage, spoke at once to the deep need in the life of the slaves. They were literalists in their interpretations, not only because such was the dominant pattern of the religious thinking of the environment, but also because their needs demanded it. It is a commonplace that what we have need to use in our environment, we seize upon; it is a profound expression of the deep self-regarding impulses at the heart of man's struggle for the perpetuation of his own rights.

Many liberties were taken with the religious ideas. For here we are dealing not with a conceptual approach to religion but with an intensely practical one based on the tragedy of great need. We shall illustrate this to better advantage in two of the meditations that follow.

Before we pass from this aspect of our discussion it is interesting to point out that the life and the mind were ever on the alert for the dramatic quality in the Bible story. The outstanding significance of the Bible was that it provided the slaves inspiration and illumination as they sought to thread life's mystery with very few clues. What they had found true in their experience lived for them in the sacred Book. God was at work in history. One of the oldest songs said:

> Who lock, who lock de lion,
> Who lock, de lion's jaw?
> God, lock, God lock de lion's jaw.

The point is relevant!

God was the deliverer. The conception is that inasmuch as God is no respecter of persons, what He did for one race He would surely do for another. It was a faith that makes much in contemporary life that goes under that name seem but filthy rags. Daring to believe that God cared for them despite the cruel vicissitudes of life meant the giving of wings to life that nothing could destroy. This is a basic affirmation of all high religion.

The Bible—Jesus of the Gospels. Few of the spirituals have to do with the nativity of Christ. This has given rise to many speculations. James Weldon Johnson was of the opinion that the fact that Christmas Day was a day of special license having no religious significance to slaves, is largely responsible. My own opinion somewhat concurs. It should be added that, in the teaching of the Bible stories concerning the birth of Jesus, very little appeal was made to the imagination of the slave because it was not felt wise to teach him the significance of this event to the poor and the captive. It was dangerous to let the slave understand that the life and teachings of Jesus meant freedom for the captive and release for those held in economic, social, and political bondage. Even now these implications are not lifted to the fore in much of the contemporary emphasis upon Jesus. It is of first-rate significance to me that Jesus was born of poor parentage; so poor indeed was he that his parents could not offer even a lamb for the sacrifice but had to use doves instead.[1] Unlike the Apostle Paul, he was not a Roman citizen. If a Roman soldier kicked Jesus into a Palestinian ditch he could not appeal to Caesar; it was just another Jew in the ditch. What limitless release would have been available to the slave if the introduction to Jesus had been on the basis of his role as the hope of the disinherited and the captive. In the teaching of the Christian religion to the slave this aspect of the career of Jesus was carefully overlooked, and continues to be even now. Much is said about what the Christian attitude toward the poor should be; but I have yet to hear a sermon on the meaning of the religion of Jesus to the disinherited, to the poor.

When I was a boy it was my responsibility to read the Bible to my grandmother, who had been a slave. She would never permit me to read the letters of Paul, except on occasion the 13th Chapter of First Corinthians.

[1] Cf. *Jesus and the Disinherited,* Abingdon Press, pp. 17ff., 1949.

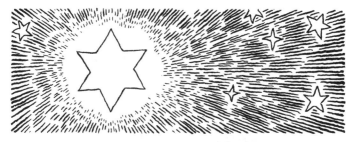

When I was older, this fact interested me profoundly. When at length I asked the reason, she told me that during the days of slavery, the minister (white) on the plantation was always preaching from the Pauline letters—"Slaves, be obedient to your masters," etc. "I vowed to myself," she said, "that if freedom ever came and I learned to read, I would never read that part of the Bible!"

Nevertheless, there are a few Christmas spirituals that point out the centrality of the significant event that took place in Bethlehem. There is one that connects the birth of Jesus with his coming into the life of the individual—an inner experience of the historical fact.

When I was a seeker,
I sought both night and day,
I asked de Lord to help me,
And He show'd me de way.

Go tell it on de mountain,
Over the hills and everywhere,
Go tell it on de mountain,
That Jesus Christ is born.

Another of these songs celebrates the star leading to Bethlehem. It is like finding the pearl of great price or

the treasure hidden in the field—for which the finder
leaves all else.

> Dere's a Star in de East on Christmas morn,
>> Rise up, shepherd, an' foller.
> It'll lead to de place where de Savior's born,
>> Rise up, shepherd, an' foller.
> Leave yo' sheep an' leave yo' lambs,
>> Rise up, shepherd, an' foller.
> Leave yo' ewes an' leave yo' rams,
>> Rise up, shepherd, an' foller.

One of the spirituals dealing with the birth of Jesus
Christ is called "Three Wise Men to Jerusalem Came."

> Sister Mary had-a but one child,
>> Born in Bethlehem.
> And-a everytime-a the-a baby cried,
> She'd-a rocked Him in the weary land.

> O Three Wise Men-a to Jerusalem came,
> They'd travelled very far.
> They said, "Where is He born, King of the Jews,
> For we have-a seen His star?"

> King Herod's heart was troubled,
> He marvelled but his face was grim;
> He said, "Tell me where the Child may be found,
> I'll go and worship Him."

> An angel appeared to Joseph,
> And gave him-a this command,—
> "Arise ye, take-a your wife and child
> Go flee into Egypt land.

> "For yonder comes old Herod,
> A wicked man and bold,
> He's slay-in' all the chillun—
> From six to eight days old."

The familiar old song, "Lit'l Boy, How Ole Are You?" belongs in this listing. No one who has ever heard him will forget the whimsical overtones produced by Roland Hayes as he sings:

Lit'l Boy, how ole are you?
    "Sir, I'm only twelve years old."

This Lit'l Boy had them to remember,
He was born the twenty-fifth of December;
Lawyers and doctors were amazed
And had to give the Lit'l Boy the praise.

Lit'l Boy, how ole are you?
    "Sir, I'm only twelve years old."

Lawyers and doctors stood and wondered,
As though they had been struck by thunder.
Then they decided while they wondered,
That all mankind must come under.

Lit'l Boy, how ole are you?
    "Sir, I'm only twelve years old."

The last time the Lit'l Boy was seen,
He was standin' on Mount Olivet green;
When He'd dispersed of the crowd,
He entered up into a cloud.

Lit'l Boy, how ole are you?
    "Sir, I'm only twelve years old."

In many of the songs the majesty of Jesus stands forth in a very striking manner; in fact, in most of the songs that treat Jesus as a religious object, he is thought of as King. In these, Jesus and God are apparently synonymous. This may have been a form of compensation, an effort to give to the spirit a sense of worth and validation, that transcends the limitations of the environment. For if Jesus, who is Saviour, is King, then the humble lot of the worshiper is illumined and lifted. The human spirit makes a dual demand with reference to God—that God be vast, the Lord of Life, Creator, Ruler, King, in a sense imperial; and that He also be intimate, primary, personal. The contrast is most marked:

> He's the lily of the valley,
>   O my Lord,
> He's the lily of the valley,
>   O my Lord,

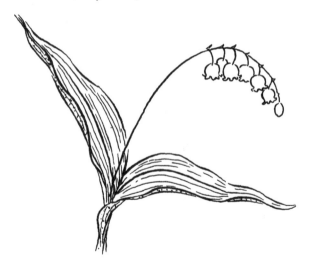

> King Jesus in His chariot rides,
>   O my Lord,
> With four white horses side by side,
>   O my Lord!

Or sense the majesty of these lines:

> He's King of Kings, and Lord of Lords,
> Jesus Christ, the first and last,
>> No man works like him.
> He built a platform in the air,
>> No man works like him.
> He meets the saints from everywhere,
>> No man works like him.
> He pitched a tent on Canaan's ground.
>> No man works like him.
> And broke the Roman Kingdom down,
>> No man works like him.

Or:

> Who do you call de King Emanuel?
> I call my Jesus, King Emanuel—
> Oh, de King Emanuel is a mighty 'Manuel;
> I call my Jesus, King Emanuel.
>
> Oh some call him Jesus, but I call him Lord,
> I call my Jesus, King Emanuel,
> Oh, de King Emanuel is a mighty 'Manuel;
> I call my Jesus, King Emanuel.

Or this:

> O ride on, Jesus, ride on, Jesus,
>> Ride on, conquering King!
> I want t' go t' hebb'n in de mo'nin'.

In the spirituals the death of Jesus took on a deep and personal poignancy.[2] It was not merely the death of a man or a God, but there was in it a quality of identification in experience that continues to burn its way deep into the heart even of the most unemotional.

[2] See my *The Negro Spiritual Speaks of Life and Death,* Harper, 1947.

The suffering of Jesus on the cross was something more. He suffered, He died, but not alone—they were with Him. They knew what He suffered; it was a cry of the heart that found a response and an echo in their own woes. They entered into the fellowship of His suffering. There was something universal in His suffering, something that reached through all the levels of society and encompassed in its sweep the entire human race. Perhaps the best of the hymns carrying the idea of completed atonement is this one:

> But He ain't comin' here t' die no mo',
> Ain't comin' here t' die no mo'.
>
> Hallelujah t' de Lamb,
> Jesus died for every man.
>
> But He ain't comin' here t' die no mo',
> Ain't comin' here t' die no mo'.

The most universally beloved of all the hymns about Jesus is the well known "Were you there when they crucified my Lord?" Sometime ago when a group of Negroes from the United States visited Mahatma Gandhi, it was the song that he requested them to sing for him. The insight here revealed is profound and touching. At last there is worked out the kind of identification in suffering that makes the cross universal in its deepest meaning. It cuts across differences of religion, race, class, and language, and dares to affirm that the key to the mystery of the cross is found deep within the heart of the experience itself.

> Were you there when they crucified my Lord?
> Were you there when they crucified my Lord?

Oh! sometimes it causes me to tremble, tremble, tremble;
Were you there when they crucified my Lord?

The inference is that the singer was *there:* "I know what he went through because I have met him in the high places of pain, and I claim him as my brother." Here again the approach is not a conceptual one, but rather an experimental grasping of the quality of Jesus' experience, by virtue of the racial frustration of the singers.

Perhaps the most famous of the songs about the Resurrection is "An' de Lord shall Bear my Spirit Hom'." The song opens with a stanza depicting a grave scene: "Dust, dust an' ashes, fly over my grave"; and ends the first part with a semi-chorus that sounds out the basic idea: "An' de Lord shall bear my spirit hom'." The successive stanzas depict the Crucifixion, Joseph's begging the body, the rolling away of the stone, and the triumphant phrase—

> De cold grave could not hold him,
> Nor death's cold, iron band.

Then they continue with the story about Mary, and the words of the angel. After each stanza there is the deeply moving refrain:

> He rose, he rose from the dead,
> An' de Lord shall bear my spirit hom'.

The idea is clear and direct—because he rose from the dead, he will bear my spirit home. He was the conqueror of death in his own life, and hence he will be able to do no less for me. This idea has been an important aspect of Christology for many, many centuries. The unusual thing about the song is the way in which it combines in one poetic unit the fact of the Resurrection, and its relevancy for the slave's own life.

The World of Nature. The world of nature furnished the spirituals much material that was readily transformed into religious truth. The materials were used solely in terms of analogy, with no effort to work out any elaborate pattern with regard to the significance of nature, and man's relation to it. Most often the characterizations are simple and to the point.

For instance, in the South there is a small worm that crawls along in a most extraordinary manner. He draws his little tail up to his head, making his body into a loop, then holding himself by his tail, he extends his head into the air and forward. He is familiarly known as an "inch worm." His movement is slow, deliberate, formal, and extremely dignified. Often with his entire body lifted, he seems uncertain as to the way to go, swinging himself from side to side in the air, until at last he lets himself straighten out on the ground.

Observing this creature in the early morning on the cotton leaf, the slave felt that here was characterized much of his own life; hence the song:

> Keep a inchin' along,
> Massa Jesus comin' by an' by,
> Keep a inchin' along like a po' inch worm,
> Massa Jesus comin' by an' by.

In the meditation "Deep River" there is a full-orbed development of analogies drawn from nature.

Religious Experience. The religious experiences of the slave were rich and full because his avenues of emotional expression were definitely limited and circumscribed. His religious aspirations were expressed in many songs delineating varying aspects of his desires. The other-worldly hope looms large, and this of course is not strange; the other-worldly hope is always available when groups of people find themselves completely frustrated in the present. When all hope for release in this world seems unrealistic and groundless, the heart turns to a way of escape beyond the present order. The options are very few for those who are thus circumstanced. Their belief in God leads quite definitely

to a position that fixes their hope on deliverance beyond
the grave. What a plaintive cry are these words:

> Don't leave me, Lord
> Don't leave me behin'.

There is desolation, fear, loneliness, but hope, at once
desperate and profound!

Even a casual bit of reflection will reveal just how
important it was for the slave to run no risk of missing
the joy of the other world. What soul-searching must
have been present in a song like this:

> Good Lord, shall I ever be de one
> To get over in de Promise' Lan'?
> God called Adam in de garden,
> 'Twas about de cool of de day
> Called for old Adam,
> An' he tried to run away,
> The Lord walked in de garden,
> 'Twas about de cool of de day,
> Called for old Adam,
> An' Adam said, "Here I am, Lord."

Such songs as:

> I want to be ready
> To walk in Jerusalem just like John.

Or:

> Oh, swing low, sweet chariot,
> Pray let me enter in;
> I don't want to stay here no longer.

and many others suggest the same basic idea. The most
plaintive and beautiful of this entire group is

> Lord, I want to be a Christian in a' my heart!

Religion was a source of consolation that had power to raise endurance to scintillating quality. It supplied a social milieu in which the lyric words were cast. Here we are not dealing with a philosophy of unyielding despair, but a clear sharing by the members of the group with each other of the comfort and strength each found in his religious commitment.

> Let us cheer the weary traveler,
> Cheer the weary traveler,
> Along the heavenly way.

The same quality is present in "Walk Togedder, Chillun."

Yet there was always present at the same time the element of solitariness, a sense of individual responsibility for life that nothing could offset. The sense of personal spiritual need was deeply voiced in the song:

> 'Tis me, O Lord,
> Standing in the need of prayer;
> It's not my brother, but it's me, O Lord,
> Standing in the need of prayer.

For sheer loneliness of heart, felt when one by one all social reinforcement in being a member of a religious community has disappeared, and the human spirit is left stranded on the shores of its own spiritual desolation, how true is the sentiment:

> And I couldn't hear nobody pray,
> O way down yonder by myself
> Couldn't hear nobody pray.

The same heart cry is sent like a shooting star in

> Keep me from sinking down
> O Lord, O my Lord,
> Keep me from sinking down.

These songs were rightfully called "Sorrow Songs." They were born of tears and suffering greater than any formula of expression. And yet the authentic note of triumph in God rings out trumpet-tongued!

> Oh, nobody knows de trouble I've seen;
> Glory Hallelujah!

There is something bold, audacious, unconquerable, here:

> Sometimes I'm up, sometimes I'm down,
> Oh, yes, Lord,

> Sometimes, I'm almost to de groun',
> Oh, yes, Lord,

> Oh, nobody knows de trouble I've seen,
> Glory Hallelujah!

Sometimes the load is so heavy that nothing is of any avail. Hope is destroyed by its feeding on itself, and yet their destiny is deliberately placed in God's hands. It was a maniacal kind of incurable optimism that arose out of great overwhelming vitality as deep as the very well-springs of life.

> I'm so glad trouble don't last alway.
> O my Lord, O my Lord, what shall I do?

Christ told the blin' man,
    to go to the pool and bathe,
O my Lord, what shall I do?

Or again:

I'm troubled in mind,
    If Jesus don't help me, I surely will die;
O Jesus, my Savior, on Thee I'll depend.
    When troubles are near me, You'll be my
        true friend.

Freedom from slavery and freedom from life were often synonymous in the thought of those early singers. With actual freedom no closer, and the years slipping away with steady rhythmic beat, death seemed the only hope. Again God is their answer:

Children, we shall be free
When the Lord shall appear.
Give ease to the sick, give sight to the blind,
Enable the cripple to walk;
He'll raise the dead from under the earth,
And give them permission to talk.

But occasionally a new note is struck—powerful and defiant.

O freedom! O freedom!
O freedom over me!
An' befo' I'd be a slave,
I'll be buried in my grave,
An' go home to my Lord an' be free.

"Steal Away to Jesus" belongs in the group of those songs that deal with release. It is release in death. The same is true of "Swing Low, Sweet Chariot."

There is at least one hymn that belongs to that moment of heartfelt realization when it finally dawned on the soul of the slave that he *was* free. Even here God is given the credit.

> "Slav'ry chain done broke at las'—
> Goin' to praise God 'til I die.

> "I did know my Jesus heard me
> 'Cause de spirit spoke to me
> An' said, 'Rise, my chile, your chillun,
> An' you too, shall be free!' "

II

THE BLIND MAN

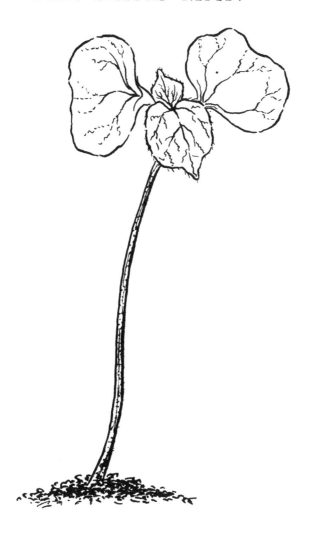

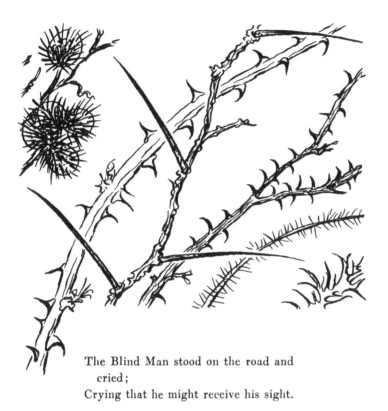

The Blind Man stood on the road and
cried;
Crying that he might receive his sight.

SINCE early morning the blind man had been waiting
by the roadside. Word had come to his village the night
before that the Healer would pass that way in the
morning. The persistent hope for sight had never quite
left him. True, he had been blind all his life, and yet,
through all the corridors of his spirit, the simple trust
persisted that he would some day gain his sight. At last,
with his head slightly tilted the better to reassure himself of the quiet thud of walking feet, he *knows*. All his
life he had waited for that precise moment. There is no

greater tragedy than for the individual to be brought face to face with one's great moment only to find that one is unprepared. Years ago I read a poem by Sara Teasdale that pictured a woman climbing a hill; all the way up she thought how grand it would be when she reached the crest, lungs full of air, a wide, almost limitless view as far as eyes could see; but "the briars were always pulling" at her gown. Then she crossed the crest; when, she did not know, for the briars were always pulling at her gown, and now all the rest of the way would "be only going down. . . ." But the blind man was ready. As Jesus approached he began crying, "Jesus, thou son of David, have mercy on me." Over and over he said it, until the words became one with the walking rhythm of the approaching feet of Jesus and his disciples. The rest of the story depicts the healing of the blind man, who goes on his way rejoicing.

The slave singers did a strange thing with this story. They identified themselves completely with the blind man at every point but the most crucial one. In the song, the blind man does not receive his sight. The song opens with the cry; it goes through many nuances of yearning, but always it ends with the same cry with which it began. The explanation for this is not far to seek; for the people who sang this song had not received their "sight." They had longed for freedom with all their passionate endeavors, but it had not come. This brings us face to face with a primary discovery of the human spirit. Very often the pain of life is not relieved —there is the cry of great desire, but the answer does not come—only the fading echo of one's lonely cry. Jesus, in the garden of Gethsemane, prayed that the cup might pass, but he had to drink it to the last bitter dregs. The Apostle Paul prayed for the "thorn" to be taken from his flesh, but he had to carry the thorn to his grave. These are but two illustrations from the early history of the church that etch in clear outline the same basic insight. For the slave, freedom was not on the horizon; there stretched ahead the long road down which there marched in interminable lines only the rows of cotton, the sizzling heat, the riding overseer with his rawhide whip, the auction block where families were torn asunder, the barking of the bloodhounds—all this, but not freedom.

Human slavery has been greatly romanticized by the illusion of distance, the mint julep, the long Southern twilight, and the lazy sweetness of blooming magnolias. But it must be intimately remembered that slavery was a dirty, sordid, inhuman business. When the slaves were taken from their homeland, the primary social unit was destroyed, and all immediate tribal and family ties were ruthlessly broken. This meant the severing of the link that gave the individual African a sense of *persona*. There is no more hapless victim than one who is cut off from family, from language, from one's roots. He is completely at the mercy of his environment, to be cowed, shaped, and molded by it at will. When the Negro

Mission of Friendship was in India several years ago, one of the things that puzzled the students and friends there was the fact that we spoke no African language and wore no distinctively African dress. Again and again they asked, "Why do you speak only the language of the conqueror? Why do you wear only Western clothes?"

Again, the slave was cut off from his religion, whatever kind it was. It is quite beside the point to say that he was given Christianity, an infinitely better religion than anything he had known before. When the master gave the slave his (the master's) God, for a long time it meant that it was difficult to disentangle religious experience from slavery sanction. The existence of these songs is in itself a monument to one of the most striking instances on record in which a people forged a weapon of offense and defense out of a psychological shackle. By some amazing but vastly creative spiritual insight the slave undertook the redemption of a religion that the master had profaned in his midst.

In instance after instance, husbands were sold from wives, children were separated from parents; a complete and withering attack was made on the sanctity of the home and the family. Added to all this, the slave women were constantly at the mercy of the lust and rapacity of the master himself, while the slave husband or father was powerless to intervene. Indeed, the whole sorry picture is a revelation of a depth of moral degradation that even in retrospect makes forgiveness one of the greatest fruits of the spirit.

Frustration with no answer in the environment! Under such circumstances, what does one do? This is

the fundamental issue raised by this song. It is quite possible to become obsessed with the idea of making everything and everybody atone for one's predicament. All one's frustrations may be distilled into a core of bitterness and disillusionment that expresses itself in a hardness of attitude and a total mercilessness—in short, one may become mean. You have seen people like that. They seem to have a demoniacal grudge against life; because they are unable to corner it and wreak their churning vengeance against it, they penalize everything else they touch. They show no favors, demand none. They trust no one and have no interest in doing so, but on the slightest provocation lash out in an almost maniacal fury. Sometimes they are less obvious, and show no emotion, but are deliberate and calculating in their attack and conquest. For them life is essentially evil, and they are essentially vengeful. "Cruel" is the word

that may describe them. They are out to settle a score with life. They have nothing to lose, because they have lost everything. This is one alternative for those who face a complete and overwhelming frustration.

Or such persons may withdraw completely into themselves. Very carefully they build a wall around themselves and let no one penetrate it. They carry the technique of detachment to a highly developed art. Such people are not happy, nor are they unhappy, but are completely indifferent. They look out on life through eyes that have burned out, and nothing is left but a dead, cold stare. Life has been reduced to routine, long ago learned by heart, and for them laid aside. There comes to mind the statue over the grave of the wife of Henry Adams in the old Rock Creek Cemetery in Washington—perhaps you have seen it. There is the seated figure of a woman whose chin is resting on her supporting right hand. The whole figure is draped in a large, inclusive fold of greenish bronze. She is looking steadily ahead, with eyes open but unseeing. The total effect is of something that is burned out—no spark is left; and yet there is a certain sense of being alive. This is the mood and tense of the person who embraces the second alternative. A great silence envelops the life, like the stillness of absolute motion suddenly stopped. A proud people irretrievably beaten in battle, who must give quarter to the occupying enemy, sometimes react this way. It is what may be called "the silence of a great hatred." Sometimes the attitude expresses itself in terms of aggressive cynicism and a pose of bold, audacious, belligerent defiance.

The final alternative is creative—thought of in terms

of a second wind. It involves the exercise of a great and dynamic will. An accurate appraisal of all circumstances is clearly seen, understood, challenged; and despite the facts revealed, hope continues even against odds and evidence. Stephen Benét depicts this very dramatically in *John Brown's Body*. There is a scene in which Lincoln is probing the universe to find the right way . . . the sure answer to his problem-urgency. He thinks of himself as an old hunting dog, whose energies are spent, "tail down, belly flattened to the ground"—he can't go

a step further. There is complete exhaustion; but the will remains, and becomes the rallying point for a new persistency that finally unlocks the door through which he moves to release and fulfillment. He goes on because he must go on.

This is the discovery made by the slave that finds its expression in the song—a complete and final refusal to be stopped. The spirit broods over all the stubborn and recalcitrant aspects of experience, until they begin slowly but inevitably to take the shape of one's deep desiring. There is a bottomless resourcefulness in man that ultimately enables him to transform "the spear of frustration into a shaft of light." Under such a circumstance even one's deepest distress becomes so sanctified that a vast illumination points the way to the land one seeks. This is the God in man; because of it, man stands in immediate candidacy for the power to absorb all the pain of life without destroying his joy. He who has made that discovery knows at last that he can stand anything that can happen to him. "The Blind Man stood on the road and cried"—the answer came in the cry itself. What a panorama of the ultimate dignity of the human spirit!

III

HEAVEN! HEAVEN!

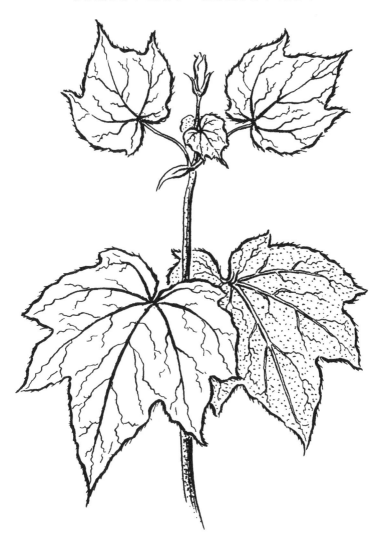

I got wings,
You got wings,
All God's children got wings.

THE setting of this spiritual is very dramatic. The slave
had often heard his master's minister talk about heaven,
the final abode of the righteous. Naturally the master
regarded himself as fitting into that category. On the
other hand the slave knew that *he* too was going to
heaven. He reasoned, "There must be two separate
heavens—no, this could not be true, because there is
only one God. God cannot be divided in this way. I have
it! I am having my hell now—when I die I shall have my
heaven. The master is having his heaven now; when he
dies he will have his hell."

The next day, chopping cotton beneath the torrid skies, the slave said to his mate—

> I got shoes,
> You got shoes,
> All God's children got shoes.
> When we get to Heaven
> We're goin' to put on our shoes
> An' shout all over God's Heaven.
> Heaven! Heaven!

Then looking up to the big house where the master lived, he said:

> But everybody talking 'bout Heaven
> Ain't going there.

This is one of the authentic songs of protest. It was sung in anticipation of a time that even yet has not fully come—a time when there shall be no slave row in the church, no gallery set aside for the slave, no special place, no segregation, no badge of racial and social stigma, but complete freedom of movement. Even at that far-off moment in the past, these early singers put their fingers on the most vulnerable spot in Christianity and democracy. The wide, free range of his spirit sent him in his song beyond all barriers. In God's presence at least there would be freedom; slavery is no part of the purpose or the plan of God. Man, therefore, is the great enemy of man. This is the mood of that song.

But there is a further problem here of critical, ethical import. The age-old technique by which the weak have survived in the midst of the strong[1] is to fool the strong. Deception, hypocrisy, lying, become the mechanism by

[1] For fuller description see chapter on "Deception," *Jesus and the Disinherited.*

which the weak protect themselves from the strong. Nature abounds in many examples of this technique for survival. The cuttlefish when attacked releases sepia fluid from its bag to make the water murky, and in this

cloud of invisibility escapes to live for yet another day. Some animals pretend to be dead when threatened. As a boy I have seen birds "play dead" when the shadow of the hawk appears on the ground. Deceive and live for yet another day, is written large in the manual of survival of many forms of life, including man. Children work out this technique in dealing with parents; students do it sometimes with teachers when lessons are not prepared. Tradition has it that women have ruled their men folks for countless ages by the simple use of this stratagem.

This is a powerful weapon of all oppressed peoples. Often they communicate with each other in a language that has a double meaning. Sometimes they resort to ciphers or simple codes or symbols. A brilliant case in point is to be found in the Book of Ezekiel. The poor, the distressed, the disinherited all over the world are using this technique to lengthen the tenuous thread by which they cling to their physical existence. They make their bodies and their minds commit to memory ways of behaving that will tend to reduce their exposure to violence. False pretense under threat poses one of the most searching ethical problems for the human spirit.

The ethical question here raised has to do with the issue of compromise. If the choice is between annihilation and survival, does that mean that deception and hypocrisy take on a moral quality that drains them of their toxin? If this is true, then perhaps there was no moral issue in the mind from the beginning. It is one of the great spiritual problems of Christianity in America that it has tolerated such injustices as between Negroes and Caucasians, for instance; that in this area of human relations its moral imperative has been greatly weakened. It is for this reason that many people all over the world feel that Christianity is weakest when it is brought face to face with the color bar.

This whole ethical problem I have expressed in a section of a prose poem on Jesus.[2]

The word—*Be genuine!*
Let your words be yea, yea; nay, nay!
All else, obscures truth,
Tempting man to betray the Eternal.
What a hard word for the weak!
It brings crashing down around their heads
The great fortress of defense
Against embattled power.
Somewhere in a past forgot,
In the first moments of internecine strife,
The weak took refuge behind deception's web,
Stretching their brittle threads of guarded life
Against odds too great to meet on equal terms.

[2] Howard Thurman, *The Greatest of These*, pp. 5ff.

46

The *will to live* made all else dim.
By circuitous route, by devious means,
Weaving a pattern of false leads and feinting starts,
Life kept itself intact
And did not die.

The little birds know this:
    Feeding in meadows under sun-drenched skies,
    The shadow of the Hawk appears.
    Time stops! all else forgot,
    Conditioned feet gather dead brown grass.
    A quick somersault and all is changed.
    High above, the Hawk clears his eyes,
    Shifts his course and seeks his meal
    In other fields.
    One with grass and root, they live
    For yet another day.

Little children know this:
    When parental will looms threateningly
        to deter or interfere,

Defiance is not wise
By route direct and unabashed!
A steely web of chaste deception
Trips and holds in firm embrace
The parental power
Until at last it yields to the little will
As if it were its own.

The weak know this:
All victims of Might
Draw from this churning source—
By the waters of Babylon they mingled tears
With flowing streams.
Into their midst Ezekiel came,
    to comfort, soothe, make unafraid.
Words like liquid fire gushed forth at eventide—
Flaming words, but hidden in a vibrant code,
Crystal clear to all with ears to hear.
Distant Tyre, and far-off Egypt named he them.
But all the biting anger of prophetic ire
Bespoke in deftest phrase of Babylon.
The Exiles knew and were consoled,
While Babylon kept watch, unconscious of the
    work the prophet wrought.
Who said, "I am God"?—
Poor old Hiram of struggling Tyre?
Hardly.
It was the mighty King of Babylon.
The captives knew and found fresh strength.
It is an age-old way the weak have found
To fight the strong with hidden tools.

But the word would not be stilled:
Let your motive be simple;
Your words, yea, yea; nay, nay.
Hypocrisy for self-defense—

Is that the sinless sin?
Does it degrade the soul at last
And sweep the raft against the hidden rocks?
Deceive, and live for yet another day!
Declare, and run the risk of sure destruction!

But why?
There is a point beyond which man cannot go,
Without yielding his right to try again.
To play God false to save one's skin,
May jeopardize all there is that makes man, Man.
"What would a man give in exchange for
his soul?"
This is the great Decision!
Even death becomes a little thing.
To survive with inner cleanness;
To compromise where ground forsook can be retrieved;
To stand unyielding when the moment comes;
This is the meaning of the Word!

One of the most serious results of this deflection is in the lives of Negroes themselves. They know from cruel experience that the Christian ethic has not been suffi-

ciently effective in the life of the Caucasian or the institutions he controls to compel him to treat the Negro as a fellow human being. It is clear, then, that there can be no hope until both the Negro and the Caucasian lift the level of their relationship to the highest point of moral and religious responsibility. Precisely this must be done if there is to be any authentic realization of spiritual, moral, and democratic freedom. The Christian ethic and segregation must forever be at war with each other.

How then may we deal with the basic issue raised by this song? There seem to be at least three alternatives, if we accept the proposition that no man can live in a social order of which he does not approve without some measure of compromise! The first alternative is to be simply, directly truthful, whatever may be the cost in life, or limb, or security. For the individual who accepts this in deed there would probably be quick and speedy judgment with attendant loss. But if the number increased and the movement spread, the vindication of truth would follow. The difficulty here is the fact that there must always be the confidence that truth will vindicate itself in the minds of the oppressor as well as of the oppressed. The greatest enemy to the wholesome response to honesty and directness in human relations is the moral apathy that results from power on the one hand and fear on the other. Direct and honest dealing make use of the technique of moral suasion and moral appeal. It is the only force admissible. It can be only effective where there are both humility and courage. Lacking either or both of these, there can be neither honesty nor directness in the relations between the strong and the weak. It is in this area and at this point that the battle of Christian ethics is either lost or won.

The second alternative is to accept as a fact that there is no alternative. This is the usual solution—the acceptance of the mood that takes for granted a facile insincerity. Morally it is chaotic. Of course the weak and the strong cannot deal honestly with each other as long as there is this differential between them. The strong know that they are going to be fooled by the weak, and their job becomes one of reducing that to ineffectiveness by a wide variety of devices. The pattern of deception by which the weak are deprived of their civic, economic, political, and social rights without its appearing that they are so deprived is a matter of continuous and tragic amazement. The pattern of deception by which the weak circumvent the strong and manage to secure some of their political, economic, and social rights is a matter of continuous and tragic degradation. A vast conspiracy of silence covers all these maneuvers as the groups come into contact with each other and the question of morality is not permitted to invade it.

The third alternative is to juggle the areas of compromise on the assumption that the moral quality of compromise operates on an ascending-descending scale.

Not all issues on this basis are equal as far as their moral decisiveness is concerned. Or it may be that some compromises take on the aspect of inevitability because of circumstances over which the individual has no possible control. Sometimes there is no choice but to live in the ghetto; sometimes Jim Crow admits of no alternative except death. But there are areas in which the margin of choice widens for the individual. There is a point beyond which we may not go in yielding for any reason whatsoever. When that moment arrives the pertinent question of Jesus, "What would a man give in exchange for his soul?" becomes the profoundest question of life. The men for whom that point never comes in his relations with his fellows has already lost his soul.

This, then, is the perpetual problem of the weak; and the issue is set in this spiritual, which has been more completely vulgarized in modern times than any other: *"Heaven! Heaven! Everybody talkin' about Heaven ain' goin' there."* No greater moral issue is before us today than this:

> To play God false to save one's skin—
> Is this the sinless sin?

Only he who faces the searing fires of that burning crucible can say either "Yea," or "Nay."

IV
A BALM IN GILEAD

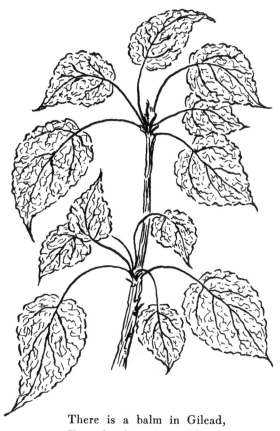

There is a balm in Gilead,
To make the spirit whole.
There is a balm in Gilead,
To heal the sin-sick soul.

THE peculiar genius of the Negro slave is revealed here
in much of its structural splendor. The setting is the
Book of Jeremiah. The prophet has come to a "Dead
Sea" place in his life. Not only is he discouraged over
the external events in the life of Israel, but he is also

spiritually depressed and tortured. As a wounded animal he cried out, "Is there no balm in Gilead? Is no physician there?" It is not a question of fact that he is raising —it is not a question directed to any particular person for an answer. It is not addressed either to God or to Israel, but rather it is a question raised by Jeremiah's entire life. He is searching his own soul. He is stripped to the literal substance of himself, and is turned back on himself for an answer. Jeremiah is saying actually, "There must be a balm in Gilead; it cannot be that there is no balm in Gilead." The relentless winnowing of his own bitter experience has laid bare his soul to the end that he is brought face to face with the very ground and core of his own faith.

The slave caught the mood of this spiritual dilemma, and with it did an amazing thing. He straightened the question mark in Jeremiah's sentence into an exclamation point: "There *is* a balm in Gilead!" Here is a note of creative triumph.

The melody itself is most suggestive. It hovers around the basic scale without any straying far afield. Only in one place is there a sharp lifting of a tonal eyebrow —a suggestion of escape; and then the melody swings back to work out its destiny within the zones of melodic agreement.

The basic insight here is one of optimism—an optimism that grows out of the pessimism of life and transcends it. It is an optimism that uses the pessimism of life as raw material out of which it creates its own strength. Many observers of Negroes have remarked that they are a happy-go-lucky people. They are quick to laugh. They are stereotyped as buffoons and clowns. What is overlooked is the fact that the basic laughter of the Negro is vital and dynamic, leaping out of an elemental faith in life itself, which makes a sense of ultimate defeat not only unrealistic but impossible. This humor

arises out of the creative unfolding of two very profound insights.

In the first place, there is the insight that life is its own restraint. The logic of this notion is that there is a moral order by which the life of the individual is bound. It is inescapable, and applies to all men alike. If this is true, men do reap what they sow; not only because it is so written in the Book, but also because it is a part of the nature of life. In the last analysis life cannot be fooled, however powerful and clever the individual may be. This notion is a dynamic weapon in the hands of the disadvantaged. It makes it possible for them to ride high to life, and particularly to keep their spirits from

being eaten away by gloom and hopelessness. The slave made this discovery long ago; this insight came to him crystal clear, and was a boon and a saviour.

Let us see how the slave's mind worked on this. The master is just a man after all, bound by the same moral laws and physical laws that bind the slave. The fact that he is in power simply increases his temptation to think that he is not bound by the same things that bind the slave. In his sense of security, made possible by the illusion of omnipotence, he forgets to be mindful of the things that ultimately bind him. The coming of the Civil War with all its tragic consequences—the laying waste of plantations, the complete destruction and disintegration of wealth, the withering of well-nigh limitless powers—the stark and gaping emptiness of the big house which once rang with laughter and joy: all these

were climactic vindications to the slaves that life is its own restraint, that no man can beat the game.

How easy it is to forget this—to think that life will make an exception in one's own case. This is a timely lesson for our nation as a whole. At the moment we stand as the graphic masters of much of the earth by virtue of our vast resourcefulness, our material resources, and the techniques by which we have reduced great conglomerates of nature to simple units of control and utility. It is a terrifying truth that life is its own restraint, and that the moral law that binds in judgment the life of the individual binds the nation and the race. Unless there is a great rebirth of high and holy moral courage, which will place at the center of our vast power an abiding sense of moral responsibility, both because of our treatment of minorities at home and our arrogance abroad, we may very easily become the most hated nation on earth. No amount of power, wealth, or prestige can stay this judgment. If we would be beloved we must share that kind of spirit as the expression of the true genius of our democratic government.

It is the fundamental realization of the notion that life is its own restraint that sustained the slave in his darkest days, and gave him an elemental vigor that expressed itself in a deep optimism arising out of the pessimism of life. He picks up the searching words of Jeremiah and sings his affirmation, "There is a balm in Gilead!" Of course there are those who may say that this is merely a defense mechanism, likened unto the mood of a man in prison who thanks God that he is there; for if he were not, he might be hit by a stray bullet. Such reflections regard this mood as a defense mechanism, which becomes a substitute for action that would relieve the pressure. The only answer to this is that there would have been no survival in this philosophy for the Negro if it were merely a mechanism of sheer defense.

The second insight here is that the contradictions of life are not in themselves either final or ultimate. This points up the basic difference between pessimism and optimism. The pessimist appraises the facts of experience, and on their face value is constrained to pass a final judgment on them. If there are contradictions between good and evil—between that which makes for peace and that which makes for turbulence—then these contradictions are regarded from this point of view as being in themselves ultimate and final; and because they are ultimate, inescapable, and therefore binding. Back of such a view is the conception that life in essence is fixed, finished, unchanging. Man is caught in the agonizing grip of inevitables; and whatever may be his chance or circumstantial assignment, all his alternatives are reduced to zero. For the man in power this is a happy philosophy. All notions of social superiority based on the elevation of a principle of racial inequality lifted to the dimension of a law of life, find their nourishment here. They state in bold terms that the God of the universe is basically partial, immoral or amoral; or, from the point of view of the underprivileged by birth or election, God is demoniacal. This undermines all hope for the oppressed, and if it is embraced gives them no sense of the future that is different from the experience of the past. The structure of the universe is stacked against them, and they may die in ultimate defiance of it, but their death will be but a futile gesture, bringing havoc to all who survive the relentless logic of such abiding fatalism.

But if perchance the contradictions of life are not ultimate, then there is always the growing edge of hope in the midst of the most barren and most tragic circumstances. It is a complete renunciation of the thoroughgoing dualism of the point of view just discussed. It is a matter of supreme significance that men are never quite robbed of all hope. There is something present in the spirit of man, sometimes even taking the

form of great arrogance, sometimes quietly nourishing the springs of resistance to a great tyranny—there is something in the spirit of man that knows that the dualism, however apparently binding, runs out, exhausts itself, and leaves a core of assurance that the ultimate destiny of man is good. This becomes the raw material of all hope, and is one of the tap-roots of religious faith for the human spirit. When it applies to the individual and becomes the norm of human relationships, a new sense of the ethical significance of life becomes manifest. Just as no man is ever quite willing—protestations to the contrary notwithstanding—to give himself up, so we are under judgment not to give each other up. The root of this judgment is found in the fact that deep within us is the conviction that man's destiny is a good destiny. To illustrate. For a period—how long we do not know but certainly ever since the memory of man became self-conscious—there has been war among men. Yet in times of even temporary cessation from struggle, or in times of greatest conflict, the dream of peace continues to nourish the hope of the race. This dream persists, even though we do not know what peace on earth would be like because it has never been experienced. We continue to hope against all evidence to the contrary, because that hope is fed by a conviction deeper than the processes of thought that the destiny of man is good. It is this spirit that has been captured by the spiritual. Yes, *"There is a balm in Gilead to heal the sin-sick soul."* The day that this conviction leaves the spirit of man, his moment on the earth is over, and the last fond hope of the race perishes from the earth forever, and a lonely God languishes while before Him His dreams go silently to dust.

V
"DEEP RIVER"

I've known rivers ancient as the
    world and older than the flow of
    human blood in human veins.
My soul has grown deep like the rivers.
I bathed in the Euphrates when
    dawns were young,
I built my hut near the Congo and
    it lulled me to sleep,
I looked upon the Nile and raised
    the Pyramids above it,
I heard the singing of the Mississippi
    when Abe Lincoln went down to
    New Orleans,
And I've seen its muddy bosom turn
    all golden in the sunset.

65

I've known rivers;
Ancient, dusky rivers;
My soul has grown deep like
    the rivers.[1]

THE fascination of the flowing stream is a constant
source of wonder and beauty to the sensitive mind. It
was ever thus. The restless movement, the hurrying,
ever-changing stream has ever been the bearer of the
longings and yearnings of mankind for land beyond the
horizon where dreams are fulfilled and deepest desires
satisfied. It is not to be wondered at that in this spiritual
there is a happy blending of majestic rhythm and poig-
nant yearning:

Deep River, my home is over Jordan;
Deep River, my home is over Jordan.
O don't you want to go to that Gospel Feast
That Promised Land where all is Peace?
Deep River, I want to cross over into camp ground.

This is perhaps the most universal in insight, and certainly the most intellectual of all the spirituals. In a
bold stroke it thinks of life in terms of a river. Of course
it must be added that to these early singers—slaves as
they were—quite practically the river may have been
for many the last and most formidable barrier to freedom. To slip over the river from one of the border states
would mean a chance for freedom in the North—or, to
cross the river into Canada would mean freedom in a
new country, a foreign land. But let us reflect on a
deeper meaning here. To think of life as being like
a river is a full and creative analogy.

[1] Langston Hughes, "The Negro Speaks of Rivers" from *The Dream
Keeper.* Copyright, 1926, 1932, by Alfred A. Knopf, Inc. and re-
printed with the permission of the publisher.

The analogy is complete in the first place because a river has a very simple beginning. The Mississippi River, for instance, rises in the northern part of the United States, fed by perpetual snows; at its source it is unpretentious, simple. It increases in momentum, in depth, in breadth, in turbulence as it makes its journey down the broad expanse of America, until at last it empties itself into the Gulf of Mexico, which, in a sense, is the triumph of its own achievement!

It is the nature of the river to flow; it is always moving, always in process, always on its way. Long ago Heraclitus reminded us that "no man bathes twice in the same stream." There seems ever to be an infinite urgency that keeps the waters on business bent. They may be caught here and there in swirling pools, or temporarily stilled behind a sudden dam, but not for long. Once again they take up their march to fulfill their destiny, to keep their tryst with the sea.

Life is like that! Life on this planet—so the scientists tell us—began its long trek across the aeons, in a simple gelatinous form in far-off ages in some primeval ocean bed. It increased in complexity, in breadth, in turbulence, through myriad forms and combinations down to the latest times. Your life and my life began as a simple form, moving through varying stages of pre-natal fulfillment, until by a great climactic spasm you and I were born. Then, once again, in simple beginning, increasing in anxiety, in turbulence, sometimes in depth, often in breadth, we make our way across the broad expanse of the years.

Our life represents essential process. It is small wonder that classic Buddhism makes so much of the experience of flux in human life. We seem always to be on our way. When I was ten years old I said that the thing I sought would come to pass when I was fifteen. When I became fifteen, it would come to pass when I was eighteen; and so on and on through the years; it is around the next turning. Life is like that. Growth is made possible in human life because of this essential characteristic.

> I shall arrive! What time, what circuit first
> I ask not; but unless God send His hail,
> Or blinding fireballs, sleet, or stifling snow,
> In some time, His good time, I shall arrive!
> He guides me and the bird. In His good time.

We are never able to do anything in quite the way we want to do it. No single experience, however great, is quite able to represent us adequately. Life is essentially dynamic and alive. It's this aliveness that guarantees and sustains all the particular manifestations of life by which we are surrounded and of which we are a part. With reference to no experience are we able to write "Q.E.D."; life is essentially unfinished. All judgments concerning experience are limited and partial. It is for this reason that in the last analysis judgment belongs with God. Even our self-judgments are limited, because we can never quite get our hands on all the materials, all the facts in each case. In any total sense we must act on the basis of evidence that is never quite conclusive.

The analogy is complete again, because of the striking relationship that the river maintains with all the banks it touches. Every bank that is touched by a river gives of itself to the water. It has no option: it is the nature of the relationship that the bank yield of itself to the river that drains it. No exceptions are allowed—there can be no substitutes. To be a bank is to give itself to the river. If I want to know the story of the Mississippi River, I need not follow it through all its meanderings across the continent; all I need do is to take a shovelful of delta sand where it empties into the Gulf, analyze it carefully, and there would stand revealed the essence of its story. Life is like that! If we think for a moment of the individual as the bank of the river and of life as the river, the analogy becomes fascinating. All our experiences leave their marks.

Or as Tennyson puts it on the lips of Ulysses:

I am a part of all that I have met.
Yet all experience is an arch wherethrough
Gleams that untravelled land whose margin
Fades forever and forever when I move.

I cannot escape. All experience is raw material that

goes into the making of me. Though my experiences shape me ultimately, yet I am not my experiences. I am an experiencer—but without my particular experiences I should not be what I am. I am what I am at any particular moment by standing on the shoulders of an infinite series of yesterdays. A man cannot be quite separated from his yesterdays. Modern psychology, mental healing, modern education, all take into account this basic fact. The amazing transformation of the material ideals, concepts, and ideologies of a whole nation in one generation is a case in point. It is the nature of life that we are kneaded and molded by our experience of life.

One of the profound insights of Jesus of Nazareth is that the history of a man's life is his judgment. This illustrates the point in an amazing dimension. He gives us a picture of the climax of human history in what is generally called the Great Judgment. It is a dramatic picture. The Judge, like some Oriental despot, sits enthroned. Before him come all the nations of the earth. "I was sick, you visited me. I was hungry, you fed me. I was in prison, you came unto me." Or, "I was sick and you did not visit me. I was hungry, you did not feed me. I was in prison, you did not come unto me." These

are the terrible words of the Judgment. But the thing that is of tremendous import here is the fact that the Judge is merely a timekeeper, a recorder. He does not arbitrarily send a man to the right or left; it is the man's deeds that do it. The Judge is almost a figurehead—the point is made so sharply. In bold, awful outline the principle is etched in unforgettable austerity— the history of a man's life is his judgment. It is the lesson of the river! "It was always a serious thing to live."

The analogy is complete, again, because a river has times of drought and times of flood. Due to a lack of rainfall, principally, the channel narrows. Rocks, the formation of certain bank contours that had been covered by the river, stand revealed without the pretense made possible by the sheltering stream. In some instances the channel becomes but a faint trickle of its former self.

Through melting snows and heavy rainfall the channel sometimes becomes swollen. The river that at one time was full of peace and quiet balance, bearing on its bosom much to sustain and make glad the life of man, becomes a wild, unrestrained monster. Reckless of consequences, impersonal to good and ill, the turbulent waters roll on their relentless way. The rising of the water is a fear-inspiring experience. Have you ever been in a flood? If you have, you've seen the waters creep slowly up the banks to the very top and beyond. There is perfect indifference to the plight of the victims—prayers, cries, cursings make no difference—the water continues to rise. It is the floodtime of the river!

Life is like that! There comes a time of dryness in life; everything seems to be at low tide. There is no sharp, tragic moment; no great or sudden draining of

one's powers—only the silent loss of enthusiasm for living. Nothing seems to matter—just a great dryness of the spirit. No great demands are made on life—there are no particular hopes on the horizon—no great anticipation or expectation lures one on. It is the time of drought. I do not mean here the reaction to tragedy or frustration. For some people it comes as a reaction to some phenomenal spurt of energy expended in achieving a special goal. Of course there are some who are dry by temperament, and who find it most necessary to keep in direct touch with some person or even some object that keeps the waters of life flowing at full channel. The time of drought may be seasonal, or it may be specially circumstanced. It is therefore of greatest importance to understand its cause, and to discover early in life what special reserves must be tapped so as to bring flowing fully and freshly the refreshing, lifegiving currents. There is perhaps no greater revelation of character than what is revealed by the things to which one appeals for regeneration, for restoration!

Life is like the river in floodtimes as well. There is something uncanny about the way in which disaster sometimes befalls the individual. One is often reminded of the words of Jesus,—"For he that hath, to him shall be given: and he that hath not, from him shall be taken even that which he hath." Here is a person whose life is moving along smoothly without deep disturbance. One is surrounded by friends and loved ones; one has reasonable comforts, good health, emotional security, and all the other things that go to make for tranquility of mind and body. Then it comes! Death to loved ones, incurable illness, loss of job, some greater deception—these and things like them converge on life, and strip one bare of all external props and securities. Out of the depths of one's frustration or alarm one may cry out that life is not good but evil; there is some basic demoniacal monster in control of the life of man—there can be no God, no sin, no future life, nothing but the survival of the fittest and every man for himself. It is the floodtime of the river. The answer to the floodtime of the river is a greater opening *to* the sea. The answer to the drought of the river is a larger opening *from* the sea. The sea is the answer both to the drought and the floodtime of the river. The meaning of all this becomes clearer as we examine the final aspect of the analogy.

The analogy is complete in the last analysis because the river has a goal. The goal of the river is the sea. The river is ever on its way to the sea, whose far-off call "all waters hear." All the waters, in all the earth, are en route to the sea. Nothing can keep them from getting there. Men may build huge dams, there may be profound disturbances of the earth's surface that throw the river out of its course and force it to cut a new channel across a bed of granite, but at last the river will get to the sea. It may twist and turn, fall back on itself and start again, stumble over an infinite series of hindering rocks, but at last the river must answer the call of the sea. It is restless till it finds its rest in the sea.

All the waters of all the earth come from the sea. Paradox of paradoxes: that out of which the river comes is that into which the river goes. The goal and the source of the river are the same! From gurgling spring to giant waterfall; from morning dew to torrential downpour; from simple creeks to mighty river—the source and the goal are the same: the sea.

Life is like that! The goal of life is God! The source of life is God! That out of which life comes is that into which life goes. He out of whom life comes is He into whom life goes. God is the goal of man's life, the end of all his seeking, the meaning of all his striving. God is the guarantor of all his values, the ultimate meaning—the timeless frame of reference. That which sustains the flower of the field, the circling series of

stars in the heavens, the structure of dependability in the world of nature everywhere, the stirring of the will of man to action, the dream of humanity, developed and free, for which myriad men, sometimes in solitariness in lonely places or in great throngs milling in crowded squares—all this and infinitely more in richness and variety and value is God. Men may be thrown from their courses—they may wander for a million years in desert and waste land, through sin and degradation, war and pestilence, hate and love—at last they must find their rest in Him. If there is that which at any time, anywhere in the universe, can ultimately withstand the divine urgency—then whatever it is that shows such strength is co-equal with God. Such a position to me is not only untenable, but is also a denial of the basic ethical monotheism that for me is the most satisfactory explanation of the meaning of life.

The source of life is God. The mystic applies this to human life when he says that there is in man an uncreated element; or in the Book of Job where it is written that his mark is in their foreheads. In the last analysis the mood of reverence that should characterize all men's dealings with each other finds its basis here. The demand to treat all human beings as ends in themselves, or the moral imperative that issues in respect for personality, finds its profound inspiration here. To deal with men on any other basis, to treat them as if there were not vibrant and vital in each one the very life of the very God, is the great blasphemy; it is the judgment that is leveled with such relentless severity on modern man.

"Thou hast made us for thyself and our souls are restless till they find their rest in thee," says Augustine. Life is like a river.

> Deep River, my home is over Jordan—
> Deep River, I want to cross over into camp ground.

VI

JACOB'S LADDER

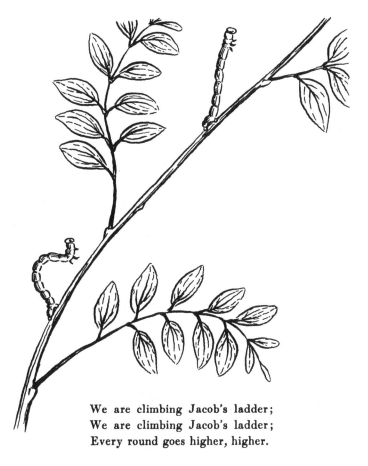

We are climbing Jacob's ladder;
We are climbing Jacob's ladder;
Every round goes higher, higher.

HAVE you ever heard a group singing this song? The listener is caught up in the contagion of a vast rhythmic pulse beat, without quite knowing how the measured rhythm communicates a sense of active belonging to the whole human race; and at once the individual becomes a part of a moving host of mankind. This is the great pilgrim spiritual.

The setting for the story is not unfamiliar to those who are acquainted with the Old Testament. Jacob had succeeded in fooling his father, and for the second time in his conspiracy, he had the added genius of his mother to assist him. When he had received the blessing from his father—a blessing intended for Esau, his brother—a mighty tension emerged between these two. Esau sought to kill him, but his mother, getting wind of this, urged Jacob to pay a visit to her brother. There seemed to be a decision on her part to make Jacob's visit face-saving. It was suggested that he seek a wife in the land in which her brother lived. Jacob set out on his journey, and when night fell he was tired. He rested on the wayside, with his head soothed by the coolness of the stone he used for a pillow. As he slept he dreamed, and in his dream behold there was a ladder stretching from earth to heaven. Moving up and down the ladder were angels, and at the top of the ladder was Jehovah. The next morning when Jacob awoke with the acute impact of the dream upon him, he said, "This is a holy place—I have seen a vision." He marked the place, as was customary, with a stone. Any passer-by seeing the stone would know that the spot had been for some man a place of encounter. Such a passer-by might honor another man's experience by adding a stone to his stone. Perhaps in time such a spot would become a shrine on which an altar would be placed.

Such is the story. Out of this picture the slave singer phrased his disturbing melody, "We are climbing Jacob's ladder. We are climbing Jacob's ladder. Every round goes higher, higher." The song gathers in its sweep all the concentrated urgencies of human dreaming.

What is the insight here? Toward what is the mind of the slave poet groping? For lack of a better and a more accurate term, it seems to me that what is being named here is the gothic principle in human life. And what is the gothic principle? It is the recognition of a two-dimensional character of reality: the giant gothic cathedral, its pillars grounded firmly in the earth and its awe-inspiring vault reaching toward the heavens. Here is the time-bound and the timeless; the finite and the infinite; the particular and the universal.

This is one of the original problems of the human spirit—as old as human thought. How can a synthesis be distilled out of the particular and the general, the finite and the infinite, the time-bound and the eternal? Wherever the human mind has wrestled with ideas and with ultimate meaning, it has tried to answer this problem. In it there is a recognition that human personality itself is the ambulating epitome of the principle we are calling the gothic. Every man recognizes that he is a creature with a body, a face, a mind; and at the same time there is something in him that always wants to fly. There is something in every one of us that tries ever to reach beyond the known, the realized, the given, the particular. The struggle seems never to be resolved; man, the earth-bound creature, with his mind and spirit moving in and out among the stars. Such is the gothic principle in human life.

We see this same principle illustrated in other practical aspects of human experience. We are never able to put into words precisely what it is that we are feeling or thinking. There is no more familiar phrase than the oft-quoted one from the Book of Hebrews, "Words fail me." The living content of experience is always richer than the articulation of experience. This is one of the reasons why the language of any people is rich in meaning and overtone. Again and again mankind tries to put into words and symbols the meanings of experience that can never quite be implied by any words or symbols, however great and strategic such words and symbols may be. A simple illustration of what I mean is in the use of the three words, "I love you." Over a period of a half century one person may say that same phrase through endless days to another person, and yet at the end of his life discover what he has known all along, that he has never been able to say what he meant.

In the great Christian doctrine of incarnation we see the heart of the problem revealed in utter starkness: the great God of the universe making Himself particular in a manifold creation, depositing awareness of this fact in limited ways in all living things and in man in particular. Finally—so the doctrine insists—He was able to particularize Himself in the man Jesus, the anointed. Thus all believers feel in this Man the achievement supreme—at last God had been able to speak Himself into time and space. Thus Jesus becomes the object of religious devotion, while he himself remains always the subject of religious experience. But here again even the believers continue to try to say who Jesus is; and no explanation is the final explanation.

There is a second suggestion inherent in the insight of this spiritual. There seems to be basic to human experience a kind of incurable optimism about the ultimate destiny of man; this is true even for people who regard themselves as confirmed pessimists. Sometimes blindly, sometimes with scarce hope of vindication, often with wild irrationality, the spirit of man dares to affirm ultimate hope. If in the present circumstances or the present world there seem to be no grounds for such assurance, there is the tendency to make immediate transfer to another period or even another form of existence or another world. This quality in human life is very important, for it is the ground of hope in times of despair, the incentive for dreams of a better day when desires are out of joint; and the "Hallelujah!" to life when worlds crash and dreams whiten into ash.

In very practical terms we see this quality at work in what out of our sophistication we may regard as the rationalizing tendency of the human mind. Here is a sick man who does not seem to be recovering according to schedule. He may say to himself, "This is the hottest summer I have ever experienced, but when the cool winds come in September I know I shall be better." And then when September comes and it is cloudy and very humid the same man may say, "What I really need is the crispness of winter." When winter comes he may say, "This is the most unseasonable winter I have ever ex-

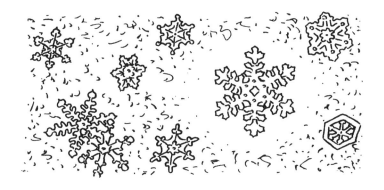

perienced. I am sure that I shall feel better in the spring." And thus it goes. When you are ten years old the thing you seek you will find when you are in your teens. When you are in your teens it will come in your twenties. And on it goes—this basic resoluteness in the human spirit that is ever the folly of basic pessimism.

The contradictions of experience, how baffling!
Moments of transcending beauty
Sicklied over by spattering ugliness;
Goodness, radiant and triumphant,
Surrounded by the persistent menace of evil, rugged and
    refined;

Love, full and uncalculating,
Struggling ever with violence, fierce and logical;
Often, so much that casts down,
Often, so little that uplifts and inspires.
The contradictions of experience, how baffling, indeed!
The final vote of man's spirit—
For what is it cast?
Does the spirit of man accept these contradictions as
    ultimate?

Does it find in them some Eternal Drama
Endless in interval, complete in meaning?
Is this apparent tension but a projection
Of what takes place deep within itself,
And all it sees is but reflection?
Or is there something more?
The final vote of man's spirit, for what is it cast?
The growing edge of hope in times of deepest despair!
The bold trust that the contradictions of life are not
    ultimate!

All this man holds against every odd—

Not merely by will and resolution,
But by processes vaster than mind,
Surer than logic,
Profounder than private plan and personal desire.
Therefore,
    All endurance finally glows in radiance!
    All hope remains forever hopeful!
    And a man can gaze without panic
    Upon the withering disillusionments of life
    With quiet eyes and peaceful heart![1]

The idea here may be briefly summarized by calling it a sense of tomorrow.

The insight of the spiritual is not only confined to the gothic principle and this sense of tomorrow, which are truly kindred notions, but there is implicit here that each man must face the figure at the top of the ladder. There is a goal. It is some kind of climax to human history. Every man must come to terms with the ultimate problem. How does he relate to something that is final in existence? In one way or another God and the human spirit must come together. Whatever things in life you believe to be true and valid, you and they must sit together in the solitude of your own spirit; and when you do what is on the agenda no form of pretension has any standing there. Even your most vaunting ambition may seem in such a moment to be

[1] Howard Thurman, *The Greatest of These*, p. 17.

filthy rags. The one searching item with which you have to deal is, how have you lived your life in the knowledge of your truth? This may not occur for the individual at the time of his dying, or at a moment of crisis, but as you turn the corner today in your own road, suddenly it is upon you. We are all climbing Jacob's ladder, and every round goes higher and higher. All who recognize this as a living part of their experience join with those early destiny-bound singers who marched through all the miseries of slavery confident that they could never be entirely earth-bound.

> We are climbing Jacob's ladder;
> We are climbing Jacob's ladder;
> Every round goes higher, higher.

VII
WADE IN THE WATER, CHILDREN

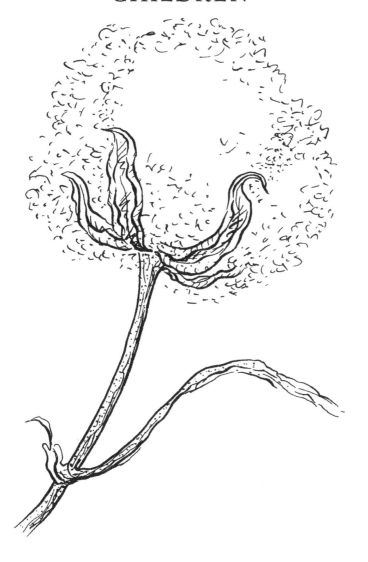

Always, patient friends placed him in the same spot beside the pool. For years longer than a fading memory could hold in focus, he had waited—this man with the incurable disease. His hope rose and fell like the ebb and flow of the ocean tide. He believed the legend, for he had seen it work its perfect work in the lives of many who had once been ill, but now were well. If somehow he could manage to be let down into the waters while they were being troubled, then *he* would be healed. No one knew precisely when the waters would be troubled; one could only wait and trust that at the miracle moment there would be someone to ease his tortured body beneath the healing waters. This is in

essence the story of the man beside the pool in the fifth
chapter of the Gospel according to St. John. What
would these early singers do with this story? They sang,

> Wade in the water,
> Wade in the water, children,
> God is going to trouble the waters.

What is the meaning of this? What are they trying
to say in these simple, insight-laden words? In the first
place they are suggesting that in all the troubles of
life, in all the experiences of life, there is an inner and
binding logic that causes the particular experience in
and of itself to be consistent; therefore rational. They
took the imagery of the simple New Testament story
and applied it to their own situation. For them the
"troubled waters" meant the ups and downs, the vicissitudes of life. Within the context of the "troubled"
waters of life there are healing waters, because God is
in the midst of the turmoil.

Here is an insistence that one must look deep within
the churning waters to find the clue to their meaning.
It is the same basic idea at this point that is disclosed
in the study of the blind man who stood in the way and
cried. Let us examine as an illustration one phase of
human experience, human illness or sickness. Consider
the study of cancer. Millions of dollars are being spent
each year in cancer research. With great versatility,
men apply in myriad ways the scientific method to the
malignant growth of cells, in the hope that the rational
principle in man may make contact with the rational
principle in the malignancy, and result in understanding, insight, and healing. All the research says that in-
herently cancer has a logic and a rational principle

operative within it. When one discovers what that rational principle is, then the resources of knowledge and wisdom and techniques can be put at the disposal of the immunizing of the organism against the ravages of the malignancy, or effectively reduce the malignancy to manageable units of control and understanding. If the disease is due to a germ, then the effort is to try to isolate the microbe, disengage it from its context, or track it down to its lair so that its habits can be understood and the conditions that bring it into being grasped and comprehended. The aim is to make available to the sufferer the deep inner resources of an ordered organism at the point of the malignancy. This very fact is a perpetual source of confidence to the seeker, that sometime he will find the clue.

This is not to indicate that to understand all this is to solve the over-all problem that human tragedy, in the form of disease, creates. The point that I am making is that there is within the disease itself a logic, a rational order, in the fulfillment of which, again and again, the private, personal plans of the individual are interrupted or even destroyed. God is troubling the waters when we are sick. Not in the sense that he causes the illness, not punishing us with sickness; but rather God is troubling the waters in human illness because inherent in the illness something rational is active, and if it is understood, its secret can be revealed so that all the overtones and creative possibilities that result from the radical interruption of one's normal processes can be turned into glorious and redemptive account. This is not mere whistling in the dark; it is not whimsical acquiescence, nor is it a shallow optimism covering a stark fear and panic. It is to say that the illness as illness can be understood;

91

then it may be dealt with in another dimension at another level, on another plane.

In the story of *The Bridge of San Luis Rey*, Thornton Wilder, with deftness and terrible insight, dismisses the engineering problem that caused the collapse of the bridge; in one creative sweep at that point he assumes a simple reasonableness. Taking that as his clue, however, he dissects the lives of the people who fell on the bridge, and shows that the same logic that was at work mechanically in the collapse of the bridge was also at work in the lives of the persons who found themselves on the bridge at that particular moment. It was all of a piece, despite the complexity of the individual lives involved. As a novelist, he could presume an omniscience with reference to the characters he created. The insight of the book, however, by inference says that if he knew the total story of any human being, the same rational principle would be the clothesline on which all the efforts of the particular life could be arranged in an orderly pattern. This sounds like the most blatant kind of fatalism; it seems to suggest that we are all of us puppets, and that some master hand moves us. I am not making that suggestion, because I do not believe that that is true. What I am saying is that in all the efforts of life, however complicated they may be if we can isolate the strands in the circumstance, we shall see that each strand in and of itself is consistent. The plaiting of the strands creates patterns that may transcend the logic of any particular strand. Always there is the order; always there is the logic. We are not altogether bound by it, because we are living, thinking, deciding creatures. In this concept there is abiding hope for man.

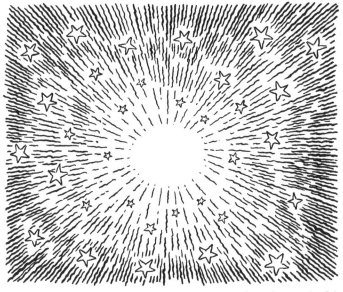

When we deal with the tragedies of life it is profitable
ever to seek to commune, to grapple with all the rational
clues that are available. It may be disclosed to me in my
search that there is nothing that I can do about it, because it is too late. Or it may be disclosed to me that
there is something that I can do, but I don't know what.
Or there is something that I can do, I know what, but I
don't know how. Or I may know what and how, but not
when. It is quite possible that a person may work at his
life problem over what for him is a total time interval,
getting more and more insight as the years unfold, with
all the richness and mellowness that such an experience
would precipitate; at last it begins to dawn deep within
the spirit that God, the creative mind and spirit in the
core of the universe, is at work.

This leads to another very searching insight. Here

we are face to face with perhaps the most daring and revolutionary concept known to man: namely, that God is not only the creative mind and spirit at the core of the universe but that He—and mark you, I say He—is love. There are no completely satisfying ways by which this conclusion may be arrived at by mere or sheer rational reflective processes. This is the great disclosure: that there is at the heart of life a Heart. When such an insight is possessed by the human spirit and possesses the human spirit, a vast and awe-inspiring tranquillity irradiates the life. This is the message of the spiritual. Do not shrink from moving confidently out into choppy seas. Wade in the water, because God is troubling the water.

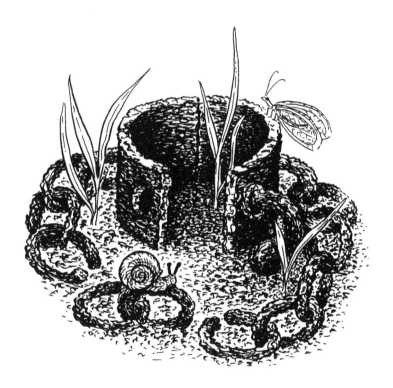

THE
NEGRO SPIRITUAL
SPEAKS OF LIFE
AND DEATH

TO

my mother and

grandmother

Preface

It has been a little more than two decades since I delivered the Ingersoll Lecture on Immortality before the Harvard Divinity School. The intervening years have witnessed the plumbing of the depths of the profound fissures that marked the hidden conflicts between the black and white brothers who are a vital part of the American family of man. What is revealed is a vast amalgam of bitterness and hatred which no one dared to acknowledge, and to admit its existence was more than the emotions could absorb or the reason tolerate. But it is a part of the living fact of the common life.

The result is a polarization of black and white, not as separate entities in a larger and inclusive continuum, but rather as two ugly monoliths animated and charged with a terrible life of their own. They are ruthless, bitter, destructive, blind to good, and fear there is no past—only a blurred future and the temporal reality of the present moment.

At such a time it is a worthy undertaking of Harper & Row to include in its J. & J. Harper Editions the reissuing of this statement of the primary discovery of the timeless reservoir of spiritual creativity and renewal which the forebears of one of the brothers made their own when their environment was completely under siege.

What they discovered was that the bitter contradictions of life are not final and that hope was built into the fabric of the struggle. This meant to them that the intensity of the tragic passage in which they were pilgrims could not be separated from the God in whom their ultimate trust was placed. Therefore, they were unwilling to scale down the horizon of their demands to the level of the existential circumstances. This was their secret, and it is this they have transmitted to their children. In the maelstrom of the present social upheaval and the fierce antagonism between the brothers, it is this Word that may redeem the times. But this cannot be done unless their children will hear their Voice above the present conflict. It is in this hope that *The Negro Spiritual Speaks of Life and Death* is reissued.

HOWARD THURMAN

Foreword

From my cabin window I look out on the full moon, and the ghosts of my forefathers rise and fall with the undulating waves. Across these same waters how many years ago they came! What were the inchoate mutterings locked tight within the circle of their hearts? In the deep, heavy darkness of the foul-smelling hold of the ship, where they could not see the sky, nor hear the night noises, nor feel the warm compassion of the tribe, they held their breath against the agony.

How does the human spirit accommodate itself to desolation? How did they? What tools of the spirit were in their hands with which to cut a path through the wilderness of their despair? If only Death of the body would come to deliver the soul from dying! If some sacred taboo had been defiled and this extended terror was the consequence—there would be no panic in the paying. If some creature of the vast and pulsing jungle had snatched the life away—this would even in its wildest fear be floated by the familiarity of the daily hazard. If Death had come being ushered into life by a terrible paroxysm of pain, all the assurance of the Way of the Tribe would have carried the spirit home on the wings of precious ceremony and holy ritual. But this! Nothing anywhere in all the myths, in all the stories, in all the ancient memory of the race had given hint of this tortuous convulsion. There were no gods to hear, no magic spell of witch doctor to summon; even one's companion in chains muttered his quivering misery in a tongue unknown and a sound unfamiliar.

O my Fathers, what was it like to be stripped of all supports of life save the beating of the heart and the ebb and flow of fetid air in the lungs? In a strange moment, when you suddenly caught your breath, did some intimation from the future give to your spirits a hint of promise? In the darkness did you hear the silent feet of your children beating a melody of freedom to words which you would never know, in a land in which your bones would be warmed again in the depths of the cold earth in which you will sleep unknown, unrealized and alone?

The Ingersoll Lectureship

Extract from the will of Miss Caroline Haskell Ingersoll, who died in Keene, County of Cheshire, New Hampshire, Jan. 26, 1893

First. In carrying out the wishes of my late beloved father, George Goldthwait Ingersoll, as declared by him in his last will and testament, I give and bequeath to Harvard University in Cambridge, Mass., where my late father was graduated, and which he always held in love and honor, the sum of Five thousand dollars ($5,000) as a fund for the establishment of a Lectureship on a plan somewhat similar to that of the Dudleian Lecture, that is—one lecture to be delivered each year, on any convenient day between the last day of May and the first day of December, on this subject, "the Immortality of Man," said lecture not to form a part of the usual college course, nor to be delivered by any Professor or Tutor as part of his usual routine of instruction, though any such Professor or Tutor may be appointed to such service. The choice of said lecturer is not to be limited to any one religious denomination, nor to any one profession, but may be that of either clergyman or layman, the appointment to take place at least six months before the delivery of said lecture. The above

[7]

sum to be safely invested and three fourths of the annual interest thereof to be paid to the lecturer for his services and the remaining fourth to be expended in the publishment and gratuitous distribution of the lecture, a copy of which is always to be furnished by the lecturer for such purpose. The same lecture to be named and known as "the Ingersoll Lecture on the Immortality of Man."

THE
NEGRO SPIRITUAL
SPEAKS OF LIFE
AND DEATH

THE mystery of life and death persists despite the exhaustless and exhaustive treatment it has been given in song and story, philosophy and science, in art and religion. The human spirit is so involved in the endless cycle of birth, of living and dying, that in some sense each man is an authority, a key interpreter of the meaning of the totality of the experience. The testimony of the individual, then, is always fresh if he is able to make himself articulate to his fellows. Even when he is not, there is the persistent conviction that in some profound sense he himself knows and understands. When the external circumstances of life are dramatic or unusual, causing the human spirit to make demands upon all the reaches of its resourcefulness in order to keep from being engulfed, then the value of its findings

[11]

made articulate, has more than passing significance.

I have chosen, coincidentally with the suggestion of Dean Sperry, to examine the Negro spirituals as a source of rich testimony concerning life and death, because in many ways they are the voice, sometimes strident, sometimes muted and weary, of a people for whom the cup of suffering overflowed in haunting overtones of majesty, beauty and power! For many years it has been a growing conviction with me that the clue to the meaning of the spirituals is to be found in religious experience and spiritual discernment. To be sure, the amazing rhythm and the peculiar, often weird 1-2-3-5-6-8- of the musical scale are always intriguing and challenging to the modern mind. The real significance of the songs, however, is revealed at a deeper level of experience, in the ebb and flow of the tides that feed the rivers of man's thinking and aspiring. Here, where the elemental and the formless struggle to a vast consciousness in the mind and spirit of the individual, shall we seek the needful understanding of the songs of these slave singers. The insights disclosed are not original in any personal or private sense. The unique factor of the inspiring revelation is that, in the presence of their naked demand upon the primary sources of meanings, even without highly specialized tools or skills, the universe responded to them with overwhelming power.

In an essay included in a little book of meditations on Negro Spirituals published under the title *Deep River*, I located three major sources of raw materials over which the slave placed the alchemy of his desiring and aspiring: the world of nature, the stuff of experience, and the Bible, the sacred book of the Christians who had enslaved him. It was from the latter two that the songs of life and death originate. An examination of some of the insights to be found here is at once the purpose and proposal of my lecture.

Death was a fact, inescapable, persistent. For the slave, it was extremely compelling because of the cheapness with which his life was regarded. The slave was a tool, a thing, a utility, a commodity, but he was not a *person*. He was faced constantly with the imminent threat of death, of which the terrible overseer was the symbol; and the awareness that he

(the slave) was only chattel property, the dramatiza-
tion. It is difficult for us, so far removed in time
and mood from those agony-ridden days, to compre-
hend the subtle psychological factors that were at
work in the relationship between slave and master.
If a slave were killed, it was merely a property loss,
a matter of bookkeeping. The notion of personality,
of human beings as ends so basic to the genius of the
Christian faith, had no authentic application in the
relationship between slave and master. The social
and religious climate were uncongenial to such an
ethic. Of course, there were significant exceptions to
the general rule—which exceptions, by the light they
cast, revealed the great moral darkness by which the
period was engulfed. The situation itself stripped
death of dignity, making it stark and nasty, like the
difference between tragedy and melodrama. Death
by violence at the hand of nature may stun the mind
and shock the spirit, but death at the hands of another human being makes for panic in the mind and
outrages the spirit. To live constantly in such a
climate makes the struggle for essential human
dignity unbearably desperate. The human spirit is

stripped to the literal substance of itself. The attitude toward death is profoundly influenced by the experience of life.

It is important then to examine this literature to see what is revealed here concerning the attitude toward death. How significant is death? Is it the worst of all possible things that can happen to an individual:

> Oh Freedom! Oh Freedom!
> Oh Freedom, I love thee!
> And before I'll be a slave,
> I'll be buried in my grave,
> And go home to my Lord and be free.

Obvious indeed is it here that death is not regarded as life's worst offering. There are some things in life that are worse than death. A man is not compelled to accept life without reference to the conditions upon which the offering is made. Here is something more than a mere counsel of suicide. It is a primary disclosure of an elemental affirmation having to do directly, not only with the ultimate

[15]

dignity of the human spirit, but also with the ultimate basis of self-respect. We are face to face with a gross conception of the immortality of man, gross because it is completely exhaustive in its desperation. A radical conception of the immortality of man is apparent because the human spirit has a final word over the effect of circumstances. It is the guarantee of the sense of alternative in human experience, upon which, in the last analysis, all notions of freedom finally rest. Here is a recognition of death as the one fixed option which can never be taken from man by any power, however great, or by any circumstance, however fateful. If death were not implicit in the fact of life in a time-space dimension, then in no true sense would there be any authentic options in human experience: This concept regards death merely as a private option, private because it involves the single individual as if he and he alone existed in all the universe; option, because, while it assumes the inevitability of death as a factor in life, it recognizes the element of time which brings the inevitable factor under some measure of control.

The fact that death can be reduced to a manageable unit in any sense, whatsoever, reveals something
that is profoundly significant concerning its character. The significant revelation is in the fact that
death, as an event, is spatial, time encompassed, if
not actually time bound, and therefore partakes of
the character of the episodic. Death not only affects
man by involving him concretely in its fulfillment,
but man seems to be aware that he is being affected
by death in the experience itself. There is, therefore,
an element of detachment for the human spirit, even
in so crucial an experience. Death is an experience
in life and a man, under some circumstances, may
be regarded as a spectator *of*, as well as a participant
in, the moment of his own death. The logic here
is that man is both a space binder and a time
binder.

The second attitude toward death that comes to
our attention is one of resignation mixed with elements of fear and a manifestation of muted dread
—this, despite the fact that there seems to have
been a careful note of familiarity with the experiences
of death. It is more difficult for us to imagine what

[17]

life was like under a less complex order of living, than is our lot. We are all of us participants in the modern conspiracy to reduce immediate contact with death to zero except under the most extraordinary circumstances. We know that death is a commonplace in the experience of life and yet we keep it behind a curtain or locked in a closet, as it were. To us death is gruesome and aesthetically distasteful as a primary contact for ourselves and our children. For most of us, when members of our immediate families die, the death itself takes place in a hospital. Particularly is this true of urban dwellers. From the hospital, the deceased is carried to a place of preparation for burial, the mortuary. When we see the beloved one again, the body has been washed, embalmed, and dressed for burial. Our exposure to the facts involved, the silent intimacies in preparation for burial are almost entirely secondary, to say the least. The hospital and the mortuary have entered profoundly into the life of modern man, at this point. The result is that death has been largely alienated from the normal compass of daily experience. Our sense of personal loss may be great but our primary relationship with death under normal circumstances tends to be impersonal and detached. We shrink from direct personal contact with death. It is very difficult for us to handle the emotional upsets growing out of our experience with death when we are denied the natural moments of exhaustive reaction which are derivatives of the performance of last personal services for the dead. Therapeutic effects are missed. Tremendous emotional blocks are set up without release, making for devious forms of inner chaos, which cause us to limp through the years with our griefs unassuaged.

This was not the situation with the creators of the Spirituals. Their contact with the dead was immediate, inescapable, dramatic. The family or friends washed the body of the dead, the grave clothes were carefully and personally selected or especially made. The coffin itself was built by a familiar hand. It may have been a loving though crude device, or an expression of genuine, first-class craftsmanship. During all these processes, the body remained in the home—first wrapped in cooling sheets and then "laid out" for the time interval before burial. In the case of death from illness all of the final aspects of the experience were shared by those who had taken their turn "keeping watch." Every detail was etched in the mind and emotions against the background of the approaching end. The "death rattle" in the throat, the spasm of tense vibration in the body as the struggle for air increased in intensity, the sheer physical panic sometimes manifest—all these were a familiar part of the commonplace pattern of daily experience. Out of a full, rich knowledge of fact such a song as this was born:

> *I want to die easy when I die.*
> *I want to die easy when I die.*
> *Shout salvation as I fly,*
> *I want to die easy when I die.*

A quiet death without the seizure of panic, the silent closing of the door of earthly life, this is the simple human aspiration here.

As if to provide some measure of contrast, the age-old symbolism of the river of death appears in a song like this:

Chilly water, chilly water,
Hallelujah to that lamb.
I know that water is chilly and cold,
Hallelujah to that lamb.
But I have Jesus in my soul,
Hallelujah to that lamb.
Satan's just like a snake in the grass
Hallelujah to that lamb.
He's watching for to bite you as you pass
Hallelujah to that lamb.

In a bold and audacious introduction of still another type of symbolism which has all the graphic quality of the essentially original, revealing the intimate personal contact with death and the dying, this old, old song announces:

Same train carry my mother;
Same train be back tomorrer;
Same train, same train.
Same train blowin' at the station,
Same train be back tomorrer;
Same train, same train.

There is a sense of the meaning of death as a form of frustration (for those who remain) with a dimension of realism rare and moving in this song:

> You needn't mind my dying,
> You needn't mind my dying,
> You needn't mind my dying,
> Jesus goin' to make up my dying bed.
>
> In my dying room I know,
> Somebody is going to cry.
> All I ask you to do for me,
> Just close my dying eyes.
>
> In my dying room I know,
> Somebody is going to mourn.
> All I ask you to do for me,
> Just give that bell a tone.

In the third place, death is regarded as release, as complete surcease from anxiety and care. This is to be distinguished from that which may come after death. We are thinking here of the significance of death regarded somewhat as a good in itself. The meaning of death in such a view is measured strictly against the background of immediate life experience. It is not a renunciation of life because its terms have been refused, but an exulting sigh of sheer release from a very wearying burden:

I know moon-rise, I know star-rise,
    I lay this body down.
I walk in the moon-light, I walk in the star-light,
    To lay this body down.
I walk in the graveyard, I walk through the graveyard
    To lay this body down.
I lie in the grave and stretch out my arms,
    To lay this body down.

Man, the time binder, one with the shimmering glory of moonlight and starlight and yet housed in a simple space-binding body, is heir to all the buffetings of the fixed and immovable, yet he can lay the body down and stretch out his arms and be at one with moonrise and starlight.

The note of the transcendence of death is never lacking—whether it is viewed merely as release or as the door to a heaven of endless joys. We shall examine the place and significance of the concepts dealing with that which is beyond death at a later point in our discussion. But the great idea about death itself is that it is not *the master of life*. It may be inevitable, yes; gruesome, perhaps; releasing, yes; but triumphant, NEVER. With such an affirmation ringing in their ears, it became possible for them, slaves though they were, to stand anything that life could bring against them.

It is next in order to examine the attitude taken toward life, because the attitude toward death cannot be separated from the attitude toward life. Was life merely a "veil of soul-making"? Was it merely a vast anteroom to the great beyond? Was it regarded as an end in itself? Or was it a series of progressions, a pilgrimage, a meaningful sojourn?

There seem to be no songs dealing with the origin of life as such or the orgin of the individual life in particular. Life was regarded essentially as the given —it was accepted as a fact without reflection as to cause or reason. They were content to let the mystery remain intact.

Given the fact of life, there is much which has to do with interpretations of its meanings, its point and even its validity. In the first place, life is regarded as an experience of evil, of frustration, of despair. There are at least two moods in evidence here—one mood has to do with an impersonal characteristic of life itself. Loneliness and discouragement—such is the way of life. One cannot escape—such experiences are inherent in the process itself. Hence:

> Let us cheer the weary traveler,
> Let us cheer the weary traveler,
> Along the heavenly way.

This has some elements similar to the philosophy of unyielding despair developed by Bertrand Russell in his essay on a Free Man's Worship.

> Sometimes I feel like a motherless child,
> A long way from home.

[25]

Here again is another song which reflects the same temper.

There is also the familiar note in:

> Nobody knows the trouble I've seen,
> Nobody knows my sorrow.
> Nobody knows the trouble I've seen,
> Glory, Hallelujah!

All the reaches of despair are caught up and held in a trembling wail in:

> I couldn't hear nobody pray,
> Oh, I couldn't hear nobody pray.
> Oh, way down yonder by myself,
> And I couldn't hear nobody pray.

A climactic chord in the mood of the seventh chapter of Paul's letter to the Romans is to be found in:

> O wretched man that I am!
> O wretched man that I am!
> Who will deliver poor me?

My heart is filled with sadness and pain,
Who will deliver poor me?

The solitariness of the human spirit, the intensely personal characteristic of all experience as distinguished from mere frustration or despair is evident in such a song as:

I've got to walk my lonesome valley,
I've got to walk it for myself.
Nobody else can walk it for me,
I've got to walk it for myself!

Here we are in the presence of an essential insight into all human experience. It seems, sometimes, that it is the solitariness of life that causes it to move with such intensity and power. In the last analysis all the great moments of profoundest meaning are solitary. We walk the ways of life together with our associates, our friends, our loved ones. How precious it is to lean upon another, to have a staggered sense of the everlasting arms felt in communion with a friend. But there are thresholds before which all

[27]

must stop and no one may enter save God, and even He in disguise. I am alone but even in my aloneness I seem sometimes to be all that there is in life, and all that there is in life seems to be synthesized in me.

It is a matter of more than passing interest that this element of overwhelming poignancy is relieved somewhat by a clear note of triumph. Out of the fullness of a tremendous vitality the lowering clouds are high-lighted by an overflowing of utter exuberance:

> *I feel like a motherless child;*
> *I feel like a motherless child;*
> *Glory hallelujah!*
> *Sometimes my way is sad and lone,*
> *When far away and lost from home;*
> *Glory hallelujah!*

The same note appears in a softer key, expressive of a quiet but sure confidence:

> *Soon-a-will be done with troubles of the world;*
> *Soon-a-will be done with troubles of the world;*
> *Going home to live with God.*

Or again the quality of triumph is to be found in the total accent of the song:

> *All-a-my troubles will soon be over with,*
> *All-a-my troubles will soon be over with,*
> *All over this world.*

The second mood suggested in the interpretation of life as an experience of evil, of frustration, of despair, has to do with a personal reaction to the vindictiveness and cruelty of one's fellows. The mood is set in a definite moral and ethical frame of reference which becomes a screening device for evaluating one's day-by-day human relations. It would be expected that these songs would point indirectly to be sure, but definitely, to the slave owner. But for the most part, the songs are strangely silent here. Many indeed have been the speculations as to the reason for this unnatural omission. There are those who say we are dealing with children so limited in mentality that there is no margin of selfhood remaining for striking out, directly or indirectly, in a frenzy of studied fury against the slave owner. This is arrant nonsense as the vast number of slave insurrections all through this terrible period will certify. There are those who say that the religion was so simple, so naïve, so completely otherworldly that no impression was made by the supra-immoral aspects of the environment; only a simple acceptance of one's fate. Any person who has talked with an ex-slave could hardly hold such a position. There seems to be a more comprehensive answer than any of these. The fact was that the slave owner was regarded as one outside the pale of moral and ethical responsibility. The level of high expectation of moral excellence for the master was practically *nihil*. Nothing could be expected from him but gross evil—he was in terms of morality—amoral. The truth seems to be that the slave owner as a class did not warrant a high estimate of ethical judgment. There is no more tragic result from this total experience than the fact that even at the present time such injunctions as "love your enemies," etc. are often taken for granted to mean the enemy within the group itself. The relationship between slave and master, as far as both the slave and the master were concerned, was "out of bounds" in terms of moral responsibility. It seems clear, then, that the second mood has to do with those "we group" relationships of the slave and his fellow bondsmen.

Such is the meaning of:

Down on me, down on me,
Looks like everybody in the whole round world is
     down on me.
Talk about me as much as you please,
I'll talk about you when I get on my knees.
Looks like everybody in the whole round world is
     down on me.

Sometimes I'm up, sometimes I am down,
Sometimes I'm almost on the ground
Looks like everybody in the whole round world is
     down on me.

To refer to the refrain of one other such song:

Oh, this is a sin-trying world,
This is a sin-trying world.

[31]

In the second place, life is regarded as a pilgrimage, a sojourn, while the true home of the spirit is beyond the vicissitudes of life with God! This is a familiar theme of the human spirit. We are dealing with a striking theory of time. Time is measured in terms of events, actions, therefore intentions and desires. All experience, then, is made up of a series of more or less intense meaning—units that may fall in such rapid succession that the interval between is less than any quantitative value. Within the scope of an event-series all of human life is bound. Freedom can only mean, in this sense, the possibility of release from the tyranny of succeeding intervals of events. The totality of life, then, in its existential aspects, is thus completely exhausted in time. Death in such a view means complete cessation of any sense of interval and therefore of any sense of events. In short, here death means either finality or complete absorption from time-space awareness. Whatever transpires beyond death, while it can be thought of only in terms of time-space intervals, is of another universe of discourse, another quality of being.

It is in order now to raise a question as to the

[32]

relation between *before* and *after* in terms of death
and life. There seems to be no real break between
before and after. Any notion of the continuity of
life that transcends the fact of death is significant
because of the advantage that is given to the meaning of life. Even though it be true that death is a
process moving toward fulfillment in a single climactic event; as contrasted with life, death seems
ever to be a solitary event; while life does not seem
to be a single event but a process. Even at birth, the
process of life seems to be well under way, well
advanced. In the light of man's conscious experience
with life, death seems to be a moment for the release
of potentials of which the individual is in some sense
already aware. Life then becomes illustrative of a
theory of time that is latitudinal or flowing. On the
other hand, death is suggestive of a theory of time
that is circular or wheel-like.

Life always includes movement, process, inner
activity and some form of irritation. Something more
is implicit than what is apparent in any cycle or series
of cycles that sustain all manifestations. In such a
view, life takes on a definite character of timeless-

[33]

ness. There are no isolated, unrelated and, therefore, inconsequential events or moments. Every day is fraught with antecedents and consequences the logic of which is *inner relatedness* rather than *outer seeming*. Every day is a day of judgment and all life is lived under a continuous and inner scrutiny.

To think of life, then, as a pilgrimage means that not only is life characterized by an undertow of continuity but also that the individual has no alternative but to participate responsibly in that continuity. It is this concept rooted in the New Testament interpretation of the meaning of life that is to be found in many of the Spirituals. A few of such songs have been mentioned in other connections. One of the great utterances of this character is:

Done made my vow to the Lord,
And I never will turn back,
I will go, I shall go,
To see what the end will be.

My strength, Good Lord, is almost gone,
I will go, I shall go,

To see what the end will be.
But you have told me to press on,
I will go, I shall go,
To see what the end will be.

The goal of the pilgrimage looms large by inference in some of the songs. The goal is not defined as such in many of them—but the fact of the goal pervades the temper with which the journey is undertaken or endured. There is something filled with breathless anticipation and great strength in these lines:

Wait a little while,
Then we'll sing a new song,
Wait a little while,
Then we'll sing a new song.

Sometimes I get a heavenly view,
Then we'll sing a new song,
And then my trials are so few,
Then we'll sing a new song.

[35]

There is no attempt to cast a false glow over the stark ruggedness of the journey. The facts of experience are seen for what they are—difficult, often even unyielding:

It is a mighty rocky road,
Most done travelling.
Mighty rocky road,
Most done travelling.
Mighty rocky road,
Bound to carry my soul to the Lord.

Hold out your light you heaven-bound soldier,
Let your light shine around the world.

Of the sheer will to carry on under the compelling aegis of a great commitment, what could be more accurately expressive than:

Stay in the field,
Stay in the field,
Until the war is ended.

[36]

Mine eyes are turned to the heavenly gate,
Till the war is ended.
I'll keep my way, or I'll be too late,
Till the war is ended.

Here is still another variation of the same basic
theme:

Oh, my good Lord, show me the way.
Enter the chariot, travel along.

Noah sent out a morning dove,
Enter the chariot, travel along,
Which brought back a token of heavenly love,
Enter the chariot, travel along.

What, then, is the fundamental significance of all
these interpretations of life and death? What are
these songs trying to say? They express the profound
conviction that God was not done with them, that
God was not done with life. The consciousness that
God had not exhausted His resources or better still
that the vicissitudes of life could not exhaust God's

resources, did not ever leave them. This is the secret of their ascendency over circumstances and the basis of their assurances concerning life and death. The awareness of the presence of a God who was personal, intimate and active was the central fact of life and around it all the details of life and destiny were integrated.

It must be borne in mind that there seems to be little place in their reckoning for the distinction between God and Jesus. In some of the songs the terms God and Jesus are used interchangeably—to illustrate:

> Did you ever see such a man as God?
> A little more faith in Jesus,
> A preaching the Gospel to the poor,
> A little more faith in Jesus.

For the most part, a very simple theory of the incarnation is ever present. The simpler assumptions of Christian orthodoxy are utilized. There was no elaborate scheme of separate office and function between God and Jesus and only a very rare reference to the Holy Spirit. Whether the song uses the term, Jesus, or the oft repeated Lord, or Saviour, or God, the same insistence is present—God is in them, in their souls, as they put it, and what is just as important, He is in the facts of their world. In short, God is active in history in a personal and primary manner. People who live under great pressures, grappling with tremendous imponderables which left to themselves they could not manage, have no surplus energy for metaphysical distinctions. Such distinctions apart from the necessity of circumstances or urgency of spirit, belong to those upon whom the hold of the environment is relatively relaxed. Urgency forces a reach for the ultimate, which ultimate in the intensity of demand is incorporated in the warp and woof of immediacy.

It is the next in order to examine the large place given to the otherworldly emphasis in these songs. What is the meaning of Heaven, of the final Judgment? In such considerations we come to grips with the conception of immortality implicit and explicit in the songs, and the basis for it.

Again and again I have heard many people (including descendants of these singers) speak disparagingly of the otherworldly emphasis as purely a mechanism of escape and sheer retreat. The argument is that such an emphasis served as a kind of soporific, making for docility and submission. It is further charged that here we are dealing with a clever device by which these people were manipulated into a position which rendered them more completely defenseless than they would have been without it.

Such an argument must be examined. In the first place, the facts make clear that religion did serve to deepen the capacity of endurance and the absorption of suffering. It was a precious bane! What greater tribute could be paid to religious faith in general and to their religious faith in particular than this: It taught a people how to ride high to life, to look squarely in the face those facts that argue most dramatically against all hope and to use those facts as raw material out of which they fashioned a hope that the environment, with all of its cruelty, could not crush. With untutored hands—with a sure artistry and genius created out of a vast vitality, a concept of God was wrenched from the Sacred Book, the

[40]

Bible, the chronicle of a people who had learned through great necessity the secret meaning of suffering. This total experience enabled them to reject annihilation and affirm a terrible right to live. The center of focus was beyond themselves in a God who was a companion to them in their miseries even as He enabled them to transcend their miseries. And this is good news! Under God the human spirit can triumph over the most radical frustrations! This is no ordinary achievement. In the presence of an infinite desperation held at white heat in the consciousness of a people, out of the very depth of life, an infinite energy took shape on their behalf.

> Oh rise, shine, for thy light is a coming.
> Oh rise, shine, for thy light is a coming.
> My Lord says he's coming by and by.

Do we wonder then that they sang:

> Oh religion is a fortune,
> I really do believe.
> Oh religion is a fortune,
> I really do believe!

In the second place, this religious emphasis did not paralyze action, it did not make for mere resignation. On the contrary, it gave the mind a new dimension of resourcefulness. I had a college classmate who cleared his throat just before responding to the question of his teacher. The clearing of the throat broke the impasse between his mind and his immediate environment so that he could have a sense of ascendency in his situation. It was in some such fashion as this that these religious songs functioned. (Of course, they did much more than this.) Once the impasse was broken, many things became possible to them. They could make their religion vehicular in terms of the particular urgencies of the moment. "Steal away to Jesus" became an important call to those who had ears to hear. In other words, far from paralyzing action, religion made for detachment from the environment so that they could live in the midst of the traffic of their situation with the independence of solitude. The pragmatic results for them was an awareness that against the darkness of their days, something warred, "a strange new courage." To them

it was the work of God and who could say to them
NAY?

We turn now to an examination of the place and significance of the notion of judgment. Taking their clue from the word picture given by Jesus in the Gospels, the Judgment was the climax of human history. This made a tremendous appeal to the imagination. The figure of Gabriel was added to the imagery of Jesus. There are many references to Gabriel:

> O get your trumpet Gabriel
> And come down on the sea.
> Now don't you sound your trumpet
> Till you get orders from me—
>
> I got a key to that Kingdom
> I got a key to that Kingdom
> And the world can't do me no harm.

To mention the refrain of one other song:

> Gabriel, Gabriel, blow your trumpet!
> My Lord says he's going to rain down fire.

Some of these songs are almost pure drama. Consider this very old hymn, no record of which is to be found in any of the available collections:

> Oh, He's going to wake up the dead,
> Going to wake up the dead,
> God's going to wake up the dead.
> One of these mornings bright and fair,
> God's going to wake up the dead.

The judgment is personal and cosmic so that even the rocks and mountains, the stars, the sea, are all involved in so profound a process:

> My Lord what a morning!
> My Lord what a morning!
> When the stars begin to fall.

> You will hear the trumpet sound
> To wake the nations underground,
> Standing at my God's right hand,
> When the stars begin to fall.

The matter of most crucial importance is this—a man is brought face to face with his own life—personal accountability is the keynote:

> When the master calls me to Him
> I'll be somewhere sleeping in my grave.
> In that great day when he calls us to him
> I'll be somewhere sleeping in my grave.

The deep intimacy between the soul and God is constantly suggested. Even the true name of the individual is known only to God. There are references to the fact that the designation, Child of God, is the only name that is necessary. This gnosis of the individual is an amazing example of the mystical element present in the slave's religious experience. The slave's answer to the use of terms of personal designation that are degrading is to be found in his private knowledge that his name is known only to the God of the entire universe. In the Judgment everybody will at last know who he is, a fact which he has known all along.

[45]

O' nobody knows who I am, who I am,
Till the Judgment morning.

Judgment takes place in time. It is a moment
when the inner significance of a man's deeds is
revealed. God shall deal with each according to his
history. It was with reference to the Judgment that
life took on a subdued character. Everybody is
judged. The Judge is impartial. There is distinct
continuity between the life on earth and the Judgment. Excuses are of no avail. God, the Judge, knows
the entire story.

O', He sees all you do,
He hears all you say.
My Lord's-a-writing all the time.

Judgment was not thought of as being immediately
after death. There is a time element between death
and final judgment. Life, death, judgment, this was
the thought sequence. When the final judgment
takes place there will be no more time. What takes
place after judgment has a necessitous, mandatory

[46]

character ascribed to it. Man can influence his judgment before death—after death everything is un-
alterable. This notion of the ultimate significance of
life on earth is another aspect of the theory of time
to which we have made reference. Here is a faithful
following of the thought of the Gospels.

And yet there is more to be said concerning the
idea of the Judgment. What does the concept say?
Are we dealing with a matter of fact and of literal
truth? If we are, then the symbolism of the Judgment
is necessarily an essential symbolism. What is the
literal truth seeking expression in this symbolism?
It is this: The life of man is significantly capable of
rising to the demands of maximum moral responsibility. That which is capable of a maximum moral
responsibility functioning in the tiny compass of
single events takes on the aspects of the beyond-
event, hence beyond time, therefore eternal. The
conclusion seems inescapable that man is inter-
preted as having only mortal manifestations, but even
these mortal manifestations have immortal overtones. If this were not true then there would be no
significance in the symbolic fact of judgment. The

[47]

literal truth requires a symbolism that is completely vehicular or revelatory.

Finally, we turn to an examination of the place and significance of the fact of Heaven in the thinking of these early singers. Heaven was a place—it was not merely an idea in the mind. This must be held in mind, constantly. The thinking about it is spatial. It is the thinking of Jesus in the Fourth Gospel. "I go to prepare a place for you. If I go and prepare a place for you I shall come again, and take you unto myself that where I am there ye may be also." "In my father's house are many mansions." These word pictures supplied a concreteness to the fulfillment of all earth's aspirations and longings. The songs are many, expressing highly descriptive language of this character:

> *I haven't been to heaven*
> *But I've been told,*
> *The streets are pearl*
> *And the gates are gold;*
> *Not made with hands.*

What a plaintive wistfulness is found here:

> In bright mansions above,
> In bright mansions above,
> Lord, I want to live up yonder;
> In bright mansions above.

Such an aspiration was in sharp contrast to dimly lighted cabins with which they were familiar. Perfection, truth, beauty, even goodness are again and again symbolized by light. This is universal.

Heaven was as intensely personal as the facts of their experience or as the fact of the Judgment. Here at last was a place where the slave was *counted in*. He had the dignity of personal registration.

> O write my name, O write my name,
> The angels in heaven are going to write my name.
> Yes, write my name with a golden pen,
> The angels in heaven are going to write my name.

Heaven is regarded as a dimension of self-extension in the sense of private possession:

[49]

I want God's heaven to be mine, to be mine,
Yes, I want God's heaven to be mine.

Who is there that can escape the irony and the triumph in:

I got a robe,
You got a robe,
All God's children got robes.
When we get to heaven
We're going to put on our robes,
We're going to shout all over God's heaven.

There will be no proscription, no segregation, no separateness, no slave-row, but complete freedom of movement—the most psychologically dramatic of all manifestations of freedom.

All of these songs and many others like them argue for an authentic belief in personal immortality. In large part it is a belief growing out of the necessities of life as they experienced it. Family ties are restored, friends and particularly loved ones are reunited. The most precious thing of all was the fact that personal identity was not lost but heightened. Heaven would not be heaven, it would have no meaning, if the fact of contrasting experiences was not always possible and evident. There was a great compulsion to know then a new and different life, which knowledge could only be real if the individual were able to recall how it once was with him. We are not surprised to find a great emphasis on reunion. There was nothing more heart-tearing in that far-off time of madness than the separation of families at the auction block. Wives were sold from their husbands to become breeders for profit, children were separated from their parents and from each other—in fact, from the beginning, the slave population was a company of displaced and dispossessed people. The possibility of ever seeing one's loved ones again was very remote. The conviction grew that this is the kind of universe that cannot deny ultimately the demands of love and longing. The issue of reuniting with loved ones turned finally on the hope of immortality and the issue of immortality turned on the fact of God. Therefore God would make it right and once again God became the answer.

This personal immortality carried with it also the idea of rest from labor, of being able to take a long sigh cushioned by a deep sense of peace. If time is regarded as having certain characteristics that are event transcending and the human spirit is not essentially time bound but a time binder, then the concept of personal survival of death follows automatically. For man is never completely involved in, nor absorbed by, experience. He is an experiencer with recollection and memory—so these songs insist. The logic of such a position is that man was not born *in* time, that he was not created by a time-space experience, but rather that man was born *into* time. Something of him enters all time-space relationships, even birth, completely and fully intact, and is not created by the time-space relationship. In short, the most significant thing about man is what Eckhart calls the "uncreated element" in his soul. This was an assumed fact profoundly at work in the life and thought of the early slaves.

This much was certainly clear to them—the soul of man was immortal. It could go to heaven or hell, but it could not *die*. Most of the references to hell are by inference. Not to be with God was to be in hell but it did not mean not to be.

It is in order to raise the same question about heaven that was raised previously about the Judgment. Are we dealing here with a matter of literal truth? Or are we once again dealing with necessary symbolism growing out of literal truth? In other words, what is the intrinsic meaning attached to or to be drawn out of the concept of heaven? Is this mere drama or some crude art form? Certain facts are quite evident in the picture given. Heaven was specific! An orderly series of events was thought to take place. The human spirit rests—the fulfillment of the exhausted. A crown, a personal crown is given —a fulfillment for those who strive without the realization of their strivings. There is a room of one's own—the fulfillment of life in terms of the healing balm of privacy. There are mansions—the fulfillment of life in terms of living with a high quality of dignity. There are robes, slippers—the fulfillment of life in terms of the restoration of self-respect. The idea at the core of the literal truth in the concept of heaven is this—life is totally right, structurally dependable, good essentially as contrasted with the moral concepts of good and evil. It affirms that the contradictions of human experience are not ultimate. The profoundest desires of man are of God, and therefore they cannot be denied ultimately.

> Our ship is on the ocean but
> We'll anchor by and by.

To use the oft-repeated phrase of Augustine, "Thou hast made us for Thyself, and our souls are restless till they find their rest in thee." There is an order, a moral order in which men participate, that gathers up into itself, dimensional fulfillment, limitless in its creativity and design. Whatever may be the pressures to which one is subjected, the snares, the buffetings, one must not for a moment think that there is not an ultimate value always at stake. It is this ultimate value at stake in all experience that is the final incentive to decency, to courage and hope. Human life, even the life of a slave must be lived worthily of so grand an undertaking. At every moment a crown was placed over his head that he must constantly grow

[54]

tall enough to wear. Only of that which is possessed of infinite potentials, can an infinite demand be required. The unfulfilled, the undeveloped only has a future; the fulfilled, the rounded out, the finished can only have a past. The human spirit participates in both past and future in what it regards as the present but it is independent of both.

We may dismiss, then, the symbolism of these songs as touching life and death if we understand the literal truth with which they have to do. The moment we accept the literal truth, we are once again faced with the urgency of a vehicular symbolism. The cycle is indeed vicious. To be led astray by the crassness, the materialistic character of the symbolism so that in the end we reject the literal truth is to deny life itself of its dignity and man the right or necessity of dimensional fulfillment. In such a view the present moment is all there is—man is no longer a time binder but becomes a prisoner in a tight world of momentary events—no more and no less. His tragedy would be that nothing beyond the moment could happen to him and all of his life could be encompassed within the boundary of a time-space

[55]

fragment. For these slave singers such a view was completely unsatisfactory and it was therefore thoroughly and decisively rejected. And this is the miracle of their achievement causing them to take their place alongside the great creative religious thinkers of the human race. They made a worthless life, the life of chattel property, a mere thing, a body, *worth living!* They yielded with abiding enthusiasm to a view of life which included all the events of their experience without exhausting themselves in those experiences. To them this quality of life was insistent fact because of that which deep within them, they discovered of God, and his far-flung purposes. God was not through with them. And He was not, nor could He be exhausted by, any single experience or any series of experiences. To know Him was to live a life worthy of the loftiest meaning of life. Men in all ages and climes, slave or free, trained or untutored, who have sensed the same values, are their fellow-pilgrims who journey together with them in increasing self-realization in

the quest for the city that hath foundations,

whose Builder and Maker is God.

Printed in the USA
CPSIA information can be obtained
at www.ICGtesting.com
LVHW041942221123
764660LV00002B/328

9 780913 408209